IT'S AN OLD
CAPE COD CUSTOM

It's an Old Cape Cod Custom

by EDWIN VALENTINE MITCHELL

Author of "It's an Old New England Custom," etc.

THE VANGUARD PRESS, INC. · NEW YORK

F
72
C3
M68

5/25/49 Removal D. 14

Manufactured in the United States of America by
H. Wolff, New York, N. Y.

29867

CONTENTS

IT'S AN OLD

CAPE COD CUSTOM

THOREAU called Cape Cod "the bare and bended arm of Massachusetts." He was not the first to use this description, but one likes to credit him with it because he visited the Cape several times and wrote what is still the best and most amusing book about it. His sandy walk along the beach from the Lights of Nauset to Cape Race was not an easy journey, and most of the way he carried as part of his luggage several volumes of local history and, quite surprisingly, an umbrella. One does not ordinarily think of an outdoor, woodsy person like Thoreau using an umbrella. Clearly he was not the man to carry one. Yet he took his to the Cape and actually used it while walking in the wind and the rain beside the sea. He seems to have managed it very well in the storm, too. There was a strong aft wind before which he sailed along the sands at a lively clip.

To many persons the seaside is only bearable when its features observe due order and proportion. They do not like sand that extends to desert vistas, nor waves of overwhelming size, nor tides that may be unpleasantly revealing. Cape Cod is almost ninety per cent pure silica, its barren lower end reminding some people of the waste lands of North Africa. The breakers on its Atlantic side, under the lash of an easterly wind, sometimes assume majestic proportions. The harbor of a fishing port like Provincetown is apt to be untidy and odorous at low tide. Yet such is the strange magic of the Cape that almost everyone who remains there for any length of time sooner or later surrenders unconditionally to its charms.

Its sandy character is perhaps the Cape's most noticeable feature. It is actually nothing but a long sand ridge, a peninsula composed almost entirely of sandy land, with groups of sand hills, some of which appear quite high, though none has an altitude of more than three hundred feet. These hills are separated by depressions and swamp country and low plains. The Cape makes out from the mainland in an easterly direction for thirty-one miles; thence turning northerly it continues for a little more than twenty miles. Its average width is five miles. It is sixty-seven miles by road from the Bourne Bridge over the Cape Cod Canal to Provincetown, sixty-two from the Sagamore Bridge. The part of the Cape between the canal at the shoulder and Chatham at the elbow is called the Upper Cape, while the remaining portion is known as the Lower Cape, sometimes also called the Hook of the Cape. The coastal country through which one approaches the peninsula is likewise generally called Cape Cod, though most people do not consider that they have reached the Cape until they have crossed the canal.

The peninsula is the easternmost county of Massachusetts—Barnstable County. It has an area of slightly more than 600 square miles, and close to 40,000 persons, not counting summer residents, dwell here. There are no cities on the Cape, only a series of fifteen small towns with numerous villages. They are not many miles apart. All the towns have English names, except Orleans which is French and Mashpee which is Indian. But many villages, localities, ponds, streams, and bays have kept their Indian designations. The number of these is unusual even for New England. Some of the towns

are of the highest American antiquity. The oldest
is Sandwich, which was settled in 1637. Barnstable,
the county seat, dates from 1639, and that same
year saw the birth of Yarmouth. Eastham was
colonized in 1644. These and the other ancient
towns of the Cape form as fine a collection of rare
and beautiful old places as can be found anywhere
in the country.

In 1849, when Thoreau visited Cape Cod for the
first time, the railroad had barely ventured onto the
peninsula, coming to an end at Sandwich; from
there he took the four-horse Concord stagecoach to
Orleans. Most people then traveled to and from the
Cape by water, for numerous fast-sailing packets
plied between Boston and the bay ports. "Every
eminence had a pole set up on it," according to
Thoreau, "with an old storm-coat or sail tied to it,
for a signal, that those on the south side of the Cape,
for instance, might know when the Boston packets
had arrived on the north."

The sandy roads made heavy going, and were
excessively fatiguing for the horses. On the Lower
Cape they waded through sand up to their fetlocks,
and often the passengers had to help by pushing
the coach. Drifting sand often obliterated the way,
and the stage driver could not tell precisely where
he had driven before. He frequently picked a new
track every day. In the lower towns the rumps of

the horses were abnormally developed from working fetlock-deep in the sand.

Provincetown was once literally a one-horse town. In 1829 Mr. Stone, the Provincetown minister, said to the schoolmaster of Wellfleet, "Would you believe that there is a town in the United States with 1800 inhabitants and only one horse with one eye? Well, that town is Provincetown and I am the only man in town who owns a horse and he is an old white one with one eye."

In those days, wheeled vehicles were seen so rarely in Provincetown that they were looked on as curiosities, particularly by the younger element in the community. Barber says that one lad, who understood navigating the ocean better than land travel, on seeing a man driving a wagon in the place, expressed surprise at his being able to drive so straight without a rudder.

Provincetown's first fire engine, which was acquired in 1836 and is now a museum piece, was equipped with extraordinarily wide wheels to prevent the apparatus from sinking in the sand. Thoreau said the wheels of the stagecoach were about five inches wide, and wagon tires on the Cape generally an inch or two wider. He even saw a baby carriage in Provincetown with six-inch tires. "The more tired the wheels, the less tired the horses," he remarked. Car drivers today who get off the hard-packed roads sometimes get stuck if the sand is soft.

The old white horse of Provincetown brings to
mind the snow-white bull which tradition says
Priscilla Mullins of Barnstable rode when she
married John Alden, to whom she made the famous
remark, "Prythee, John, why don't you speak for
yourself?" There being no horses available, Alden
substituted a bull,

Led by a cord that was tied to an iron ring in its
        nostrils,
Covered with crimson cloth, and a cushion placed
        for a saddle.

In this way the young cooper brought his bride
from Barnstable to Plymouth.

In 1827 Provincetown had only three trees. They
were willows grown from slips brought home by
a whaling captain from a tree at Napoleon's grave
in St. Helena. It must have been quite the usual
thing for visitors to that island to carry away such
souvenirs, as more than once I have come across
mementos made of the Napoleonic wood. Once in
the window of an antique shop in Shepherd Market, London, I saw a light-colored snuff box with
an engraved silver plate on the lid, saying the
box had been made from the wood of a weeping
willow growing beside the emperor's grave. Another
time, in a Philadelphia shop, I saw a walking stick
also made from a piece of this St. Helena wood.

A visitor to Provincetown in 1875 reported willows, poplars, and balm of Gilead trees of good size standing about in odd corners, as well as some ill-nourished fruit trees. In the front yard of some of the houses were lilacs, syringas, pinks, and geraniums growing in imported earth.

Viewing the sandy region of the Lower Cape has led some people to doubt the Puritan testimony that they found here "a spit's depth" of excellent black earth. Certainly the Cape had a different appearance when the Pilgrims first beheld it in 1620. For it was then forested down to the water's edge, "with oaks, pines, sassafras, juniper, birch, holly, vines, some ash, walnut." Probably not much of this was tall timber, but smaller stuff, exhibiting the usual pattern of trees exposed to the madder moods of wind and weather.

Some dead remnants of this primeval forest were still visible at the end of the eighteenth century. Dr. Belknap in his account of Provincetown (1791) says of the sea of sand hills behind the town, "This volume of sand is gradually rolling into the woods with the winds, and as it covers the trees to the tops, they die. The tops of the trees appear above the sand, but they are all dead. Where they have been lately covered the bark and twigs are still remaining; from others they have fallen off; some have been so long whipped and worn out with the sand and winds that there is nothing remaining but the hearts and knots of the trees; but over the greater part of the desert the trees have long since disappeared."

For most people the great stretch of dunes along the Lower Cape has a strange fascination. President Timothy Dwight of Yale College declared these sand hills were novel and sublime and more interesting than could be imagined. Remarking that the fine, light, yellowish sand was the sport of every wind, he said, "It is blown into plains, vallies, and hills. The hills are every height from ten to two hundred feet. Frequently they are naked, round, and extremely elegant, and often rough, pointed, wild, and fantastical, with all the varied forms which are seen at times in drifts of snow."

Henry Beston, whose book, *The Outermost House*, is a Cape Cod classic, mentions the occasional autumn sandstorms experienced along the remoter reaches of the Cape. He was out in one when "the whole world of beach and dune was one screaming, smoky, inhuman arabia of flying sand." The Coast Guard beach patrols would rather be out at night in a northeaster than in one of these dry sand blizzards.

Violent winds raising and hurling great quantities of sand against everything standing in the way for hours at a time account for frequent changes in the landscape. Ever since the sand became a menace measures have been taken to check it. In

the eighteenth century the inhabitants of Provincetown were required to cut brush to spread on the
sand, and the systematic planting of beach grass
was first undertaken more than a century ago. The
ponds have also served as a protection to the towns.

One of the most remarkable features of the Cape
is the extraordinary number of these fresh-water
ponds. There are no fewer than one hundred and
seventy-four having an area of ten acres or more,
to say nothing of a host of smaller ones. Of these,
twenty-one are over one hundred acres in extent,
and three measure upward of seven hundred acres.
They are distributed throughout the length of the
Cape, every town having at least five, with Barnstable carrying off the honors with twenty-seven.
All are less than one hundred feet above sea level,
the highest being Peter's Pond in Sandwich with an
elevation of about ninety feet. Undoubtedly some of
those near the shore were originally inlets of the
ocean which became silted up and sealed off, the
rainfall in time turning their salt contents fresh.
Thoreau, with his passion for ponds, missed the best
ones by passing along the bay shore to the Lower
Cape without visiting the wonderful sequence of
ponds beginning at Long Pond in Falmouth and
taking in Coonemosset, Ashumet, John's, Mashpee,
and others as far as Lake Chequaquet in Barnstable.
The largest of the Cape ponds is Mashpee, which is
also generally considered the most beautiful.

The sand dunes of Truro made it possible for the town militia to deceive the British regulars during the Revolution. A landing party from the fleet in the bay making for the north part of the town near Pond Village saw what appeared to be company after company of soldiers marching over the dunes as if to take up positions from which to oppose their landing. But in reality it was just a handful of men who marched over a dune in plain sight of the sea and disappearing into a hollow quickly circled the hill and marched over again in endless procession, like an army of theatrical supers who march across the stage and then run round behind the scenes to march across again to give the illusion of numbers. The British commander, seeing what appeared to be a large force on hand to meet him, decided it was unwise to attempt a landing and withdrew.

An interesting Indian legend connected with the Cape's tawny sands is that of a giant named Maushope, who used to sleep on the Cape because when he lay down to rest the shape of it suited him. But once he had a bad night. He thrashed around a good deal and in the morning found his moccasins full of sand. Taking off first one and then the other, he emptied them by flinging the contents out to sea, thereby creating the islands of Nantucket and Martha's Vineyard.

From this legend it is reasonable to conclude that the sands of the Cape are like those of the islands, but whether they actually are the same I am not qualified to say. I have read that the sands of Barnstable County differ from those along the Atlantic coast to the southward, the Cape sands being almost unadulterated silica, while iron oxides and other minerals are more prevalent in the others. The sands of Staten Island, for example, contain serpentine feldspar and even mica. A writer in the *Scientific American* some years ago explained the difference by saying that the Cape Cod sands had been longer exposed to the separative action of winds and water, had undergone far more violent intervals of translation, and were less immediately subject to replenishment by continental drainage.

Many persons, including Thoreau, have supposed the reason glass was made on the Cape at Sandwich was because of the illimitable supplies of sand available. But the Sandwich glassworks did not use any of the local sand; all of it was brought from New Jersey and the Berkshires. The reason for locating the business on the Cape was the plentiful supply of firewood to feed the furnaces.

The Cape has always been well-wooded and still is for the most part, except at its frustrated lower end. It is a mistake to think of it as a barren and monotonous land. There are beautiful trees in Sandwich, Barnstable, Yarmouth, and Dennis, which did not suffer the loss of so many in the hurricane of 1938 as did the towns on the south side of the Cape. Many trees and shrubs thrive in the sandy soil and salt air, and like all flowers that flourish near the sea, those on the Cape are of a deeper color than the same varieties grown inland. Even in exposed situations near the water the shifty character of the sand has been repressed and the bareness and glare relieved with ground covers of beach grass, beach pea, beach wormwood, and bearberry. Mass plantings of bayberry and clumps of beach plums have improved the surroundings of some places, and effective use has been made of shadbush and holly.

The people of the Cape are experienced gardeners and know what perennials and annuals do best in the sandy soil. They know that only low-growing flowers can be planted in places exposed to the sea winds, but as they usually have protected places too, there is plenty of variety in the Cape gardens. Roses seem to like the fog, and Cape Cod is noted for its ramblers. It is only right and proper that this should be the case, since it was at the famous Fay rose garden in Woods Hole that the rambler rose was originated by Michael Walsh.

There is an interesting garden note in Thoreau's *Cape Cod*. "When you express your surprise at the greenness of a Provincetown garden on the beach, in a dry season, they will sometimes tell you that the tide forces the moisture up to them. It is an interesting fact that low sand-bars in the midst of the ocean, perhaps even those which are only laid bare at low tide, are reservoirs of fresh water at which the thirsty mariner can refresh himself. They appear, like huge sponges, to hold the rain and dew that fall on them, and which, by capillary attraction, are prevented from mingling with the surrounding brine."

According to an old saying, if you once get the sand of the Cape in your shoes you will return. It is hardly possible to avoid doing this; when Thoreau left the Cape he took with him not only his umbrella and his volumes of local history, but a gill of sand in his shoes as well. He returned.

FISHING is a very ancient and vital industry. Edward Winslow states in his narrative that when representatives of the Puritans, who were then in Holland, sought the permission of King James to migrate to America, that monarch asked, "What profit might arise?" The answer was, "Fishing." Whereupon the king replied, "So, God have my soul, 'tis an honest trade; 'twas the apostles' own calling."

Cape Cod was named in 1602 by Bartholomew Gosnold from the "great store" of codfish which he took there. The Indians, according to Champlain, fished for cod in the bay with a bone hook attached to a line made of bark. But the better-equipped Pilgrims had no luck fishing during the weeks the *Mayflower* was at Provincetown while the exploring parties were out. "For cod we assayed," Mourt says in his *Relation*, "but found none; there is good store, no doubt, in their season. Neither got we any fish all the time we lay there, but some few little ones on the shore. We found great mussels, and very fat and full of sea-pearl; but we could not eat them, for they made us all sick that did eat, as well sailors as passengers."

The Pilgrims, however, liked trading better than fishing, and within a few years had established trading posts at Cape Cod and on the Maine coast. They had a better opportunity to enrich themselves than any later colony, but Samuel Adams Drake says that it was the policy of the English adventurers or backers of the enterprise to keep them poor, and he questions whether they developed the shrewdness in traffic for which their descendants became renowned. In any case, it was fur rather than fish they were chiefly interested in at first.

When the ship *Fortune*, which reached Plymouth in November, 1621, was homeward bound she was waylaid by a French man-of-war and plundered of five hundred pounds' worth of beaver belonging to the Pilgrims. In 1627, they built the Atuxcet Trading Post on the Cape in what is now the town of Bourne. It was conveniently situated between Cape Cod Bay and Buzzards Bay, and here they traded with the Indians from the Narragansett country and with the Dutch from New Amsterdam. Fur figured largely in the transactions, with wampum as the medium of exchange. A replica of this early Yankee trading post, which was established a decade before the first white settlement on the Cape at Sandwich, stands on the site of the original building. It was apparent even then that a canal across the isthmus would be a useful thing.

Fishing, however, was to outrank fur trading. The sacred wooden codfish which hangs high under the domed ceiling of the State House in Boston has served since Revolutionary times as a symbol of the importance of the fisheries to New England. They were the first successful colonial industry. They constituted the chief business of the northern colonies. At the time of the Declaration of Independence the cod fisheries furnished nearly half the money sent to England in payment of goods. Quantities of fish were exported to France, Spain, and Portugal, and a vast amount was consumed at home. So vital were the fisheries considered that, at the close of the Revolution, when peace was being negotiated with England, Massachusetts wanted no peace unless the freedom of the fishing grounds was secured to this country. It was in token of this sentiment that the codfish was hung in the State House.

John Adams of Massachusetts, who was one of the Peace Commissioners, was awake to the importance of the fisheries in the national economy, and though the negotiations were nearly wrecked over the question of fishing rights, he and his colleagues succeeded in winning the freedom of the grounds. It was stipulated in the treaty of 1783 that American fishermen could continue to visit the waters they had been accustomed to fish.

It was plain from the first that the destiny of the people settling on Cape Cod lay upon the sea, and in the period between the Revolution and the Civil War practically all the male inhabitants went to sea, either as fishermen or mariners. The cultivation of the land was left chiefly to the very old and the very young. Even the boys took to the water at an early age, but they were usually engaged in short fishing trips, and so had time to help with the work at home. Some were not more than ten when they began going out, and were full-fledged fishermen at fourteen. From the fishing fleets many of them went into the whalers and merchantmen, visiting the world's most distant seas. And many a

Cape Cod lad was captain of a ship before there was any afforestation on his cheeks.

Captain Elijah Cobb, one of a long roster of distinguished shipmasters from Brewster, went to sea as cabin boy and cook at the age of fifteen. He was born in 1768; his father died at sea in 1774, leaving his mother practically penniless with six young children. The year of the peace treaty with England, Elijah went to Boston, carrying his possessions in a liquor case, and soon succeeded in getting a berth in a vessel clearing for Surinam. At twenty-six he was in command of a ship bound for the Mediterranean, or "up straits" as such a voyage was termed. He successfully evaded the Algerian pirates, but fell into the hands of the French, who took him and his ship into Brest. Cobb set out for Paris, where he saw Robespierre, from whom he secured the release of his ship, never dreaming he would later be a witness to the guillotining of the revolutionary leader. In his book, *Memoirs of a Cape Cod Skipper*, Captain Cobb tells of his rum-running activities on the Irish coast and other sea-going adventures over a period of thirty years. The years before the War of 1812 were troublesome ones for American ships engaged in foreign trade, but Captain Cobb showed great resourcefulness in getting out of difficulties. Later he had a successful political career at home as town clerk of Brewster, representative, senator, and inspector general. He was an able navigator and a shrewd Yankee trader who succeeded in making a fortune. The Georgian-style house with a captain's walk on the roof which he built in 1800 is still standing in Brewster.

The risks involved in a seafaring life were constantly brought home to the people of Cape Cod. A bad storm always created a new crop of widows and orphans, so it is small wonder that some families migrated inland in the hope that their sons would not be tempted to go to sea. The town of East Hampton, Connecticut, for example, was settled by people from Eastham on the Cape, who wanted to keep their boys at home. But East Hampton—the name should be spelled as one word, but long usage has made it two—lies close to the Connecticut River, which leads to Long Island Sound, and the sea was in the blood streams of the Cape youths. There was no keeping them at home.

One of the worst disasters in the annals of the Cape was the historic gale of October 3, 1841, which caught the fishing fleet at George's Bank. A number of Truro vessels foundered at sea with the loss of fifty-seven men. Between forty and fifty vessels were wrecked on the Atlantic side of the Cape alone, where fifty bodies were recovered. The town of Dennis lost twenty-six of her young men in the storm, eighteen of whom had been school-mates.

At sunset on Saturday, October 2, there was a

light northeasterly wind which freshened throughout the evening until at midnight it was blowing
a gale. It continued all day Sunday, reaching its
maximum force about two o'clock Monday morning. So terrific was the gale that vessels had their
sails torn to shreds and their masts and spars carried
away. Most of the Truro vessels which had been at
or near the southwest corner of George's Bank
headed home Saturday night, but strong currents
carried them off their course to the southeast, and
seven were destroyed on Nantucket shoals with the
loss of their crews.

One fishing vessel, the *Garnet* of Truro, commanded by Captain Joshua Knowles, was not with
the fleet, but left Provincetown on Saturday and at
sunset while fishing about three miles offshore
spoke with the *Vesper* of Dennis, homeward bound
from George's Bank. The *Vesper* reported good fishing, and Captain Knowles of the *Garnet* decided to
run down and try it, not realizing he was heading
into a storm. At ten o'clock that night it was blowing hard and the light sails were taken in and at
twelve the mainsail was furled. At four in the
morning they took in the jib. As the water then
showed a depth of thirty-four fathoms they thought
they were on George's. At six o'clock Sunday morning, with the storm still increasing, they double-
reefed the foresail, which soon gave out, but was
promptly repaired and reset. A tremendous sea

carried away the boat and davits. Soundings now revealed that they were drifting toward Nantucket shoals and, in order to keep clear of them if possible, they put on more sail, adding to the reefed foresail a balance-reefed mainsail and reefed jib. The foresail now gave way again, and had no sooner been mended and reset than it was blown to pieces. Shortly afterward the same thing happened to the mainsail, leaving only the jib.

"It was now eight o'clock Sunday evening," reads an old account, "and they could do nothing more to save themselves. They sounded and found that the water measured fifteen fathoms. They then knew that they were rapidly drifting into shoal water. At the next throw of the line it measured only six fathoms. The sea was breaking over the vessel fore and aft, and the captain advised the crew to go below. All but the captain and his brother did so. They remained on deck, and after discussing the situation, concluded to swing the craft off before the wind, that, if by any possibility they were nearing land, they might have a better chance of escape. The helm was put up, and just as she began to fall off, a tremendous sea, or a breaker, completely buried the vessel, leaving her on her broadside, or beam ends. Zach, the captain's brother, was washed overboard, but he caught hold of the main sheet and hauled himself on board. The foremast was broken about fifteen feet above deck, the strain on the springstay hauled the mainmast out of the step, and tore up the deck, sweeping away the galley, bulwarks and everything else, and shifted the ballast into the wing. A sharp hatchet had always been kept under the captain's berth, to be used in case of an emergency. This he soon found, and to it fastened a lanyard, which was tied to a rope that had already been fastened to Zach's waist, the other end being secured on the vessel. Zach went to the leeward, and when the vessel rolled out of water, he watched his chance, and cut away the rigging. The captain did the same forward, cutting away the jib-stay and other ropes, and by that means relieved the vessel of the spars, sails, rigging, sheet anchor and chains. The crew got into the hold through the lazaret, and threw the ballast to the windward, so that she partially righted. They were now on a helpless wreck."

With the passing of the mammoth wave, the action of the sea became more regular. By morning there was a marked abatement in the gale. Repairs were made to the deck and the remaining anchor put out as a drag. The appearance of the water showed that they had evaded the shoals and were off soundings. Tuesday morning the weather was fair and the storm over. A schooner was sighted, but they failed to attract her notice. Sails were rigged to the stump of the foremast, so they could steer the *Garnet*. On opening the hatches, some potatoes were found floating in the hold. The galley had been swept away, but they found the teakettle in the cabin, and in this they boiled the potatoes over a fire built on the ballast. These potatoes were the first food they had tasted since Sunday morning.

Shortly before sunset a ship was seen approaching from the eastward. Signals were made and the ship bore down upon them. A boat was sent to the wreck and the crew of ten men with most of their personal effects taken off the *Garnet*. The boat then returned for the captain and the rest of the luggage. It was decided to sink the derelict; Captain Knowles chopped a hole in the bottom of the *Garnet*, which sank as he pulled away.

The rescuing ship turned out to be the *Roscius*, a famous fast-sailing packet on the New York and Liverpool run. She was bound for New York with four hundred cabin and steerage passengers. Her commander was a Truro man, Captain John Collins, who was not only related to Captain Knowles by marriage, but had been his nearest neighbor in Truro. Captain Collins's nephew, Joshua C. Paine, also of Truro, was one of the officers on the *Roscius*. Captain Knowles was surprised to meet his old Cape Cod friends at sea, but even more amazed to learn that he had been rescued two hundred miles off Neversink, New Jersey. Needless to say, the shipwrecked mariners were well treated aboard the *Roscius*, which reached New York on October seventh. Here they were also kindly and generously cared for, and not long after all hands arrived safely at Truro.

People who go down to the sea in ships are usually pretty well pickled in superstition. A disastrous storm like the one just noted seldom occurred without someone having previously dreamed about it or having had some premonition concerning the casualties. Marvelous tales of the verification of dreams are part of the folklore of Cape Cod and the seacoast of New England generally. Yet it is not surprising that seafaring populations should be prone to superstitious beliefs; from the very nature of their calling fishermen and mariners have since ancient times encountered strange phenomena and met with incidents of a mysterious and inscrutable kind.

One of the most persistent of the old superstitions is the one about the voyage begun on Friday. Setting sail on that day has long been considered unlucky, even though it has been pointed out that, so far as American seamen are concerned, historical precedents should dispel any dread of sailing then. Columbus set sail from Spain on Friday, discovered land on Friday, and came to anchor at Palos on Friday. It was on a Friday that Cabot sighted the American continent, and Bartholomew Gosnold, who visited Cape Cod eighteen years before the Pilgrims arrived, sailed from England on Friday, made the land on Friday, and reached home on Friday. Notwithstanding these instances, many a hard-headed Cape Codder found it easier to defer to the Friday superstition than to defy it, and refused to sail on that day.

Nor did Cape Codders in earlier days put to sea on the Sabbath, as that was a desecration of the holy day, and those who did so were disciplined. In 1653, Josiah Hallet and Thomas Gage of Sandwich were complained of for putting forth from Sandwich Harbor on the Lord's day. Sunday was generally observed on board Cape Cod fishing vessels while at sea. It was all right to catch fish for food on the Sabbath, but not to make a business of it. The women of the Cape liked to have their sons ship on "Sunday-keeping" vessels under skippers who did not allow card playing and similar idle amusements on the Sabbath. One of the worst things you could do on board a vessel on the Lord's day was to drive a nail. This, like whistling on shipboard, was believed likely to bring on a gale.

It was, by the way, an old Cape Cod custom to pray in meeting for anyone about to set sail on a voyage. A note was handed to the minister with the name of the person leaving home. It is related of the Reverend Josiah Dennis of Dennis that when he exchanged pulpits one Sunday with the minister of Eastham, he found on the desk a large number of these notes. Looking through them he found there were only two family names. So, holding them in his hand as he rose to pray, he said, "Here is a parcel of Cooks and Cobbs desiring the prayers of this church and congregation, being bound to sea."

A popular superstition was that if a single bird should light on a vessel, as they sometimes will when blown far from land, no good luck could possibly result from the voyage. So strongly was this belief held that vessels actually put back, and then set out on a different trip. A successful secondary voyage following such a change naturally encouraged belief in this odd omen.

Many superstitions were peculiar to certain sea areas or were personal to a particular skipper, but one which received wide acceptance was that if anything went wrong at the launching of a vessel, or if she stuck on the ways, bad fortune would always attend her. If the fact were known, men would not sail in her, and the owner was likely to have difficulty selling the vessel, or, at least, getting a fair price for her. It made no difference that some ships proved happy exceptions to this grim rule, the belief still held sway. And a person as well as a ship could acquire the reputation of being a Jonah.

There is the case of the Truro captain who had a reputation for making successful voyages. His neighbor, who had played in hard luck for several seasons, approached him with the request that he be permitted to ship with him the following season.

"I will let you know in a few days," said the skipper.

He thought the matter over, and knowing the unfortunate man was a worthy sort, who lived in a crazy old house with his sick wife and numerous children and was further burdened with debt, informed him he could go and share in the profits of the venture.

Several days later he met one of his old crew. "I hear, skipper," said the man, "that you have signed Uncle Wiff to go next year. I won't go in the vessel with him. He's a Jonah and won't make anything. You won't make a dollar, and I am not going with you if you carry him."

"I have told Uncle Wiff he could go," the captain replied, "and go he shall, make or break, whether you go or not."

It proved to be the best voyage the skipper ever made and Uncle Wiff the best man he ever had. Uncle Wiff continued to go with him until his wife recovered and he built a new house.

Another superstition believed everywhere was that it was bad luck to turn over a hatch covering. Just why this should be so is difficult to fathom, but the even more prevalent notion that it bodes ill when rats leave a vessel has a basis in sound sense. Rats dislike getting their feet wet and will abandon a ship when an abnormal leak develops. Discovery that the rodents are departing is an indication of unseaworthiness in a vessel.

Horseshoes were considered lucky, provided they were nailed in position with the points up so the luck would not run out. The customary place for affixing one was at the end of the bowsprit. Many Cape Cod vessels sported an auspicious horseshoe.

Deeply embedded in the sea lore of the Cape was a repugnance to bootjacks on vessels. No good luck could come to a vessel as long as there was one on board. This superstition worked something of a hardship on the men who had a struggle to get their fishing boots off, whether their footgear was wet or dry. The costume of the old-time fisherman generally consisted of a tarpaulin hat and monkey jacket or guernsey frock, a stout leather apron called a barvel, and ponderous fishing boots of an astonishing breadth of beam. The boots were made of the thickest russet cowhide, with tops that turned up over the knees; though extremely heavy and cumbersome, they kept the wearer's legs and feet warm and dry. Ashore, the fisherman wallowing about in his great boots was a very awkward and clumsy animal. But much as he might need the aid of a jack to divest himself of his boots, the presence of one on board a vessel was strictly taboo.

The general aversion of seafaring folk to cats on shipboard does not seem to have been fully shared by the people of the Cape. At any rate, during the later days of sail a cat was frequently part of the company on coasters, though in earlier times it was not thought safe to have one aboard.

Cats, of course, were supposed to be the pets of witches, and while there were never any witch hangings on Cape Cod, there were certainly many who believed in witches. There is a story of Captain Sylvanus Rich of Truro who, having taken on a cargo of corn for Boston in North Carolina, was held up by bad weather. Just before putting to sea, he had gone ashore and had bought a pail of milk from an old woman. This woman he blamed for the fearful gale he presently encountered off Cape Hatteras. The storm, which was moving up the coast, blew all the canvas out of Captain Rich's ship, and continued to blast the vessel until it had drifted almost to the Grand Banks. Throughout the dark terror of the storm, Captain Rich, convinced that the old crone in North Carolina was responsible for the mischief, experienced the most terrifying hallucinations. He became like a sick man, worn out in body and spirit. He solemnly informed his crew that every night the witch entered his cabin through the lazaret, and after bridling and saddling him, rode him over the sand dunes and through the woods of Truro and around Bound Brook Island.

"I can't stand it much longer," he cried.

The crew did their best to persuade him that he was deluded, but he wouldn't listen to reason. Their

situation became desperate, but while drifting help-
lessly on the wreck of their vessel, they fell in with
another ship commanded by the captain's son, Sylvanus, Jr., who soon put things to rights. He convinced his father that he was not bewitched; the
spell was broken and he was himself once more. He
put his vessel in order and they proceeded on their
voyage without further mishap, but it was a narrow
escape from disaster.

Today, Cape Codders are no more superstitious
than people elsewhere. But superstition is so deeply
rooted as to be almost a human instinct, and it may
be doubted whether it will ever die. Some of the
age-old beliefs connected with the sea still survive,
though people are usually chary of admitting the
fact.

Some fishing trips took the men from home for
long periods of time. A trip to the Grand Banks
lasted from three to five months. The fitting out of
the vessels began the first of April. They were run
on the beach to be calked and graved. The graving
process consisted of giving the bottom a coat of
pitch and burning it down with a tar barrel; this
resulted in a smooth and glossy finish. During the
early part of the nineteenth century, painted
bottoms were extremely rare. After a vessel had
been calked and graved, the sails were bent and
the stores taken aboard. After curing the fish,
which was always done in the fall when the pre-

vailing wind was northwest and there were no flies, the cured fish had to be marketed, which meant another voyage and further absence from home.

In the days of hand-lining for mackerel, sharp lines were drawn between the lucky and unlucky skippers, and the smart fisherman and the less skillful hands—the high liners and the low liners. Every man and boy aboard a fishing vessel was appraised according to his ability to catch mackerel. The standard was the average share, but in almost every crew there was usually a high liner who could get almost two shares, while the low liner was catching half a share. And a man's fishing abilities were known at home, where his merits as a fisherman sometimes affected his social relations.

There were many persons engaged in the fisheries who were kept fully occupied on shore building vessels, outfitting them, curing fish on shares, and procuring bait. This last occupation was hard work, but whole families, young and old alike, turned to it for their livelihood. The following is from an account of the town of Orleans in the year 1802.

"Clams are found on many parts of the shores of New England, but nowhere in greater abundance than at Orleans. Formerly five hundred barrels were dug here for bait; but the present year 1000 barrels have been collected. Between one and two hundred of the poorest of the inhabitants are em-

ployed in this business; and they receive from their
employers three dollars a barrel for digging the
clams, opening, salting them, and filling the casks.
From twelve to eighteen bushels of clams in the
shell must be dug, to fill, when opened, a barrel. A
man by this labor can earn seventy-five cents a day;
and women and children are also engaged in it. A
barrel of clams is worth six dollars; the employers,
therefore, after deducting the expense of salt and
the casks, which they supply, still obtain a handsome profit. A thousand barrels of clams are equal
in value to six thousand bushels of Indian corn, and
are procured with no more labor and expense.
When therefore the fishes, with which the coves of
Orleans abound, are also taken into consideration,
they may justly be regarded as more beneficial to
the inhabitants, than if the space which they occupy was covered with the most fertile soil."

Fishermen are great yarners, and one of the
greatest of story tellers was old Hutta Dyer of
Truro, among whose tales was one about bass fishing from the shore on the ocean side of the town.
Not meeting with any luck, he half-hitched his
line around his great toe and stretched out on the
sand to enjoy a brief "quish." He was soon fast
asleep, and the next thing old Hutta knew he was
being dragged feet first into the surf. He might have
been towed out to sea, but he managed to get hold

of his line and land a huge sixty-pound bass on the beach.

Bass fishing is still one of the most popular Cape pastimes, attracting scores of anglers when the stripers are biting. More than three hundred years ago William Wood wrote of the "stately basse," which he declared "one of the best fishes in the country, for tho' men are soon wearied with other fish, yet they are never with basse; it is a delicate, fine, fat, fast fish having a bone in his head, which contains a saucerful of marrow sweet and good, pleasant to the palate and wholesome to the stomach. When there is great store of them we only eat the heads, and salt up the bodies for winter, which exceed ling or heberdine. Of these fishes, some be 3 & 4 ft. long. The fisherman taking a great codline to which he fastens a piece of lobster, throws it into the sea—the fish biting at it he pulls her towards him and knocks her on the head with a stick. These are, at one time, when alewives pass up, to be caught in rivers; in lobster times, at the rocks; in mackerel times, in the bays; at Michaelmas, in the seas. When they used to tide it in and out to the rivers and creeks, the English at the top of high water do cross the creeks with long seines or basse-nets which stop the fish and the water ebbing from them, they are left on the ground sometimes 2 or 300 at a set."

Fishing, of course, is not so important an industry

on the Cape now as it was once. In Provincetown
during the summer there are probably three artists
to every fisherman. But for the artist fond of nautical subjects there are still plenty of wharves, boats,
anchors, and other nautical accessories to paint, to
say nothing of the sea and the sky and the queer
bleached country of the dunes.

For a fair span of years—one hundred and
seventy-seven, to be exact—Cape Cod has had an
unsolved murder mystery, a case of homicide on the
high seas which took the lives of three Chatham
men and a boy.

It appeared that on November 15, 1772, Captain
Joseph Doane, soon after sailing from Chatham,
sighted the schooner *Abigail* showing signals of dis-
tress. On boarding the vessel, he found only one
man, Ansell Nickerson of Chatham, who was a very
badly frightened individual, with a horrifying tale
to tell. The *Abigail* had sailed from Boston for Chatham, according to Ansell, and at two o'clock the
next morning had been overhauled by a topsail
schooner. Fearing that he would be impressed, Ansell had let himself over the stern at the end of a
rope. Four boats came with armed men, he said,
and Captain Thomas Nickerson, Elisha Newcomb,
and another man were murdered, and William
Kent, Jr., a boy of thirteen, was carried away. He
heard talk of burning the vessel, but finally she was

left to drive out to sea with her sails standing. When the pirates left, he came on deck, but found none of the crew and saw marks of blood.

Captain Doane reported that the decks were bloody, the chests broken open and plundered. A rum barrel had the head knocked out of it and only two or three gallons were left. Word was sent to the governor in Boston and Admiral Montagu put to sea immediately in the frigate *Lively* in search of the pirates. His Majesty's ships at Newport were also notified.

Meanwhile, Ansell, who had been held in the Barnstable jail, was brought to Boston. When the *Lively* returned without seeing any pirates and it was considered certain there were none on the coast, he was remanded for trial for murder on the high seas. The first trial in April resulted in a disagreement, the second trial in August in a verdict of not guilty. No trace of the four missing persons was ever found, and what actually happened on the *Abigail* remains a mystery.

Daniel Webster was struck by the very great number of sea captains, as well as other mariners, in Barnstable County. He said that frequently on the Cape he had conversed with persons who were as familiar with the Galapagos Islands, the Sandwich Islands, and remote places in the South Seas, as with the counties of Hampshire and Berkshire in Western Massachusetts.

"I was once engaged in the trial of a cause in your district," he said in a letter written in 1851 to a group of his Cape friends, "in which a question arose respecting the entrance into the harbor of Owhyee, between the reefs of coral guarding it on either side. The counsel for the opposite party proposed to call witnesses to give information to the jury concerning the entrance to that harbor. I at once saw a smile which I thought I understood; and I suggested to the judge that very probably some of the jurors had seen the entrance themselves; upon which seven out of the twelve rose and said they were quite familiarly acquainted with it, having seen it often."

The middle decades of the nineteenth century covered the clipper ship era. Perhaps the most famous of the Cape Cod clipper captains was Captain Asa Eldredge of Yarmouth, who commanded the *Red Jacket* when she made her record-breaking run between New York and Liverpool. Built by George Thomas at Rockland, Maine, from the plans of Samuel A. Pook of Boston, the *Red Jacket* measured 251 feet in length, 44 feet in breadth, and had a hold depth of 31 feet. Her registered tonnage was 2,306 tons. She was named for the Seneca Indian chief, Segoyewatha, nicknamed Red Jacket from his scarlet coat. The coat was a gift from an English army officer for aid and comfort given by Segoyewatha to the British during the Revolution, but

when the War of 1812 broke out, the chief supported the American cause. The ship's figurehead
was a full-length painted wooden image of the
chief, a much better piece of sculpture than the
usual cigar-store Indian, and on the stern amid
elaborate gold-leaf foliations was a bust of the old
chief.

The *Red Jacket* was launched at Rockland on
November 2, 1853. "No expense had been spared
in furnishing her inboard and outboard with the
best," says William Hutchinson Rowe in his *Maritime History of Maine*. "The after cabin was furnished in rosewood mahogany, satin, and zebra
wood which was set off by black walnut and gilt
work. Exclusive of the officers' quarters, with the
forward cabin there were fourteen staterooms. And
the forward house accommodated a crew of sixty-
two men. A week after launching she was towed to
New York, where she received her masts and spars,
was rigged and her sails bent."

The *Red Jacket* sailed from New York for Liverpool on her maiden voyage January 10, 1854. Her
crew was not notably efficient; she experienced
typical North Atlantic weather all the way, with
rain, hail, or snow almost every day; but despite
all handicaps the crossing was made in thirteen
days, one hour, and twenty-five minutes, dock to
dock. This is still the world's record for a sailing
ship. The day the *Red Jacket* logged four hundred

and thirteen miles Captain Eldredge let the crew "splice the main brace."

Crowds were on hand to greet the ship on her arrival at Liverpool. She came up the harbor under her own canvas in a spanking northwest breeze and was brought about and laid alongside the head of the dock in so perfectly executed a feat of seamanship that it drew cheers from the throng. She came in so fast that the pair of tugs which had managed to get lines to her could not take up the slack.

The *Red Jacket* was immediately chartered by the White Star Line, and under Captain Eldredge again astonished the maritime world by making the round trip from Liverpool to Melbourne in five months and four days. A frequently reproduced oil painting of this beautiful clipper shows her among the icebergs off Cape Horn on her memorable Melbourne run. Like his ship, Captain Eldredge had a long and distinguished career.

The Cape Cod skippers took pains to bring up the rising generation in the traditions of the sea. One of the unique features of the Cape clippers was the system of apprenticeship by which boys were trained to be future officers. These youngsters, who were generally relatives or friends of the captain or owners, were called ship's cousins, and were housed in specially built quarters amidships, where they messed apart from the crew. They were taught navigation and practical seamanship, and many of them became shipmasters.

From the very beginning Cape Cod men took a leading part in the development of American sea trade. An outstanding Cape navigator of the eighteenth century was Captain John Kendrick, a giant of a man, endowed with enormous physical strength and as fearless as he was strong. He was born in Harwich in 1740, and went whaling when he was twenty-one. During the Revolution, he was in command of several privateers, a pursuit which demanded boldness, cool judgment, and consummate seamanship, all of which he possessed. After the war he was active in developing the maritime fur trade in the Pacific, heading the expedition of the *Columbia* and the *Washington*, which sailed from Boston in the autumn of 1787. He spent some time in the *Washington* trading along the northwest coast between the island of Nootka and the Queen Charlotte Islands. He then went to the Hawaiian Islands and China, visiting Japan on his return. He was the first to take the American flag to Japan, but he was unable to do any business with the Japanese. Nor did his dream of trading in pearls and sandalwood in the Hawaiian Islands materialize. Back on the northwest coast, he continued trading in sea otter skins. At Queen Charlotte Islands he beat off a fierce onslaught of the Indians who tried to take the *Washington*. He became the owner of thousands of acres of land on Vancouver Island, but nothing came of this speculation. He revisited China in 1793, and the following year decided on a further Chinese voyage, but he never got there. Stopping at the Hawaiian Islands, he became involved in an interisland war that was then raging. His side won, but he was accidentally killed by a fellow trader while the *Washington* lay at anchor in Honolulu Harbor. Captain Kendrick asked Captain Brown of the *Jackal* to salute his ship. Captain Brown complied, but unfortunately one of his guns was still loaded, and the ball crashed through the side of the *Washington*, killing Captain Kendrick who was sitting at the table in his cabin. Thus the end came for this seagoing pioneer on December 12, 1794.

The world changes, old customs die, and Cape Codders no longer go down to the sea in ships as they once did, but just living on the Cape is as good as a sea voyage.

"A SHIP ashore and all hands perishing!"

This cry in the village streets of Cape Cod always made the men spring to their feet and hasten to the beach. It was a cry often heard in the days of sail, when the Cape was the dread of mariners, and a storm was generally sure to make it the scene of numerous shipwrecks, accompanied by loss of life.

Countless vessels have come to grief on the treacherous sands of the Cape, especially on the broad oceanside along the fifty-mile stretch between Monomoy and Race Point. There are no rocks here, but a series of constantly shifting sand bars. The outer range of these shoals lies half a mile or more offshore, the inner range perhaps a furlong or so from the land. Large, heavy ships used to strike on the outer bar even at high water and, unless a ship could be lightened enough by cutting away the masts or jettisoning the cargo to get over this bar, she was beaten to pieces and only her fragments reached the shore. Smaller vessels passed over the outer bar at full sea, and when they touched the bar at low water beat over it when the tide rose, coming close inshore, where the crews had a better chance of reaching the beach. During a severe storm a terrific cross sea runs between the two ranges of shoals, and many a ship's crew has perished trying to get ashore from the outer bar through this sea. Cape Cod was the last place on the Atlantic seaboard where a sailor would choose to be wrecked.

Wild stories used to be told of the wreckers of the Cape, who decoyed ships ashore by the use of false lights. Mooncussers they were called, because the moon interfered with their business, and they cursed it. But there was more fiction than truth in the tales that were told of these wreckers and their inhuman treatment of shipwrecked crews. Many Cape Cod men have risked and even given their lives trying to rescue others from the sea. In the old history books it is not unusual to come across paragraphs similar to the following one, which tells of an incident that occurred when the bark *Josepha* was wrecked near Highland Light in April, 1852.

"Jonathan Collins, who had just risen from the tea-table, procured the lighthouse dory, and against the entreaties of the people present started out in the boat to carry a line to the wreck. David D. Smith took his watch from his pocket and handed it to a neighbor, but as he was about to step into the boat to go with Collins, a brave young man, named D. H. Cassidy, only twenty-three years old, who had been married but a few days, shoved Smith aside and took his seat in the boat. They pushed out into the mountains of foaming waters, on through the raging seas, until they had got within about fifteen yards of the wreck, when the boat capsized, and both men perished."

From earliest times there have been men who have resorted to the beaches of the Cape in the hope of finding something of value left by the sea. Indeed, beachcombing or wrecking was a recognized means of livelihood. The Atlantic side of the Cape after a storm was often so strewn with wreckage that it resembled one of the beaches of Salvador Dali, peopled with anthropomorphic chests of drawers, old bull fiddles, secondhand pianos, and store-window dummies. All sorts of things were harvested from the shore by the beachcombers or wreckers, for whom an ill wind more often than not blew good. If they could get aboard a wreck, they swarmed out to it across the sands like vultures to a corpse and picked it clean, but not before those on board had been rescued.

Wreckers were supposed to report to the authorities valuable property salvaged from wrecks, so that it could be advertised, but this was not often done. So much property was stolen from the brig *Wilkes*, which was wrecked on the oceanside of Eastham in 1777, that the town held a meeting and appointed a committee "to detect and bring to justice, if possible, any persons who had committed this robbery, and take measures to clear the character of the town in this affair."

Probably no shipwreck ever caused more rejoicing on Cape Cod than that of the British man-of-war *Somerset*, a famous seventy-four, which came ashore north of the Clay Pounds on the further reaches of the Cape, November 8, 1778. The *Somerset* was well known to the people of the Cape, as she had been in American waters a number of years, and was one of the ships that covered the landing of the British troops at the Battle of Bunker Hill. Constantly hovering about the Cape, the *Somerset* for long periods rode at anchor in the bay halfway between Provincetown and Pond Landing at Truro. Her commander, Captain Bellamy, over-looked no opportunity to annoy the people. His barges and boats were always on the prowl. Instead of paying the inhabitants when he levied on them for fish, butter, and eggs, he sent his chaplain ashore to preach to them.

The *Somerset* came to her end on the fatal sands of the Cape while being chased by some French men-of-war. A strong north wind was blowing as the British frigate sought to make Provincetown Harbor. Failing to weather the Cape, she tacked, but misstayed, and struck on the outer bar. The French ships stood in as close as they dared, fired a few shots at her, and turned away. A heavy sea was running on the bar which smashed the *Somerset's* boats before they could get clear, causing the loss of many lives. The wreckage of the masts which had broken off short was cleared away, and many of her heavy guns and quantities of shot were thrown overboard to lighten her. Crowds watched from the beach, where the local militia had hastily assembled, and at high tide they saw the *Somerset* drive over the bar and come ashore.

The four hundred and eighty prisoners were taken to Barnstable on the first leg of their long march to Boston. The ship's surgeon, Dr. William Thayer, who was paroled, remained on the Cape, practicing in Provincetown and Truro and eventually marrying Susan Rich of the latter town.

People came from all over the Cape to see the *Somerset* and get what they could from the wreck. Josiah Paine, author of *A History of Harwich* (1937), says that a party of Harwich men who went to view her returned with souvenirs. Samuel Eldridge obtained a large set of hinges from the shutter of a porthole which within the historian's memory were to be seen on the doors of his barn. But it was the Truro and Provincetown people who got the bulk of the loot. General Joseph Otis wrote: "From all I can learn, there is wicked work at the wreck, riotous things. The Truro and Provincetown men made a division of the clothing, etc. Truro took two-thirds and Provincetown one-third. There's a plundering gang that way." Nevertheless, several of the guns which remained on the *Somerset* were salvaged by the authorities for use in defense of the Cape.

When Thoreau was at Truro more than seventy years after the stranding of the *Somerset,* he was told of a silver watch, accidentally left behind by one of the prisoners, which was still going to tell the tale. Still later, the wreck which had been buried in the sand was partly exposed when the wind blew the sand away, and several cartloads of sound oak were cut from the ship's timbers. Many souvenirs, such as ship models, watch charms, etc., were made from the wood. This was not the first time the wreck had been uncovered and it may not be the last. Some of her bones are still buried in the sand.

Captain Bellamy of the *Somerset* was not the only commander of that name to be shipwrecked on Cape Cod. Samuel Bellamy, the pirate, was driven ashore there during a violent easterly storm on Saturday, April 26, 1717. His ship, the *Whidah,* which carried twenty-three guns and was manned by one hundred and thirty men, was battered to bits by the huge waves and most of the crew drowned. So severe was the storm that the sea cut its way completely across the Cape, severing the lower end and creating a passage from the ocean to the bay through which a whaleboat passed. This was the first Cape Cod canal, but it did not last long, as the people filled it in again.

Bellamy had met with some success cruising in New England waters. He had captured seven vessels which yielded a fair amount of plunder. Shortly before the storm he had taken a vessel, which he put in charge of a prize crew of seven men. These pirates promptly drank themselves into insensibility and the captives retook the ship and deliberately let her drive ashore on the ocean side of the Cape near Truro. When she struck, it was a case of every man for himself and in the confusion the pirates escaped. But they were soon caught and eventually made to do their dance in the air without music.

Bellamy's own vessel grounded off Wellfleet. One version of the story is that the pirate promised the captain of the prize vessel a present of the captured craft if he would pilot him into Cape Cod Harbor; but suspecting that Bellamy would not keep his word and that his intention might be to sack Provincetown, the captain disobeyed orders. As it was a dark night, a lantern was hung in the shrouds of the smaller vessel for the pirates to follow. Approaching close to the land, the large pirate ship struck on the outer bar, while the lesser vessel passed over this and hit much nearer the beach. Still another version is that the captain who was supposed to pilot the pirates into Provincetown threw a burning tar barrel overboard which drifted ashore and lured the pirates into shoal water. In any case, all but two of those in the *Whidah* perished. Captain Cyprian Southack, who was detailed by the provincial government to take charge of the situation, collected and buried in the sand the bodies of one hundred and two pirates. Captain Bellamy seems to have been among the drowned.

Uncle Jack Newcomb, the Wellfleet oysterman with whom Thoreau stayed, told his guest that he had seen the iron caboose of the ship on the bar at an unusually low run of tide. Thoreau and others picked up ancient coins near the scene of the wreck. During the Civil War, nearly a century and a half afterward, the wreck was again revealed.

There is an old wives' tale told on the Cape about one of the escaped pirates from the *Whidah,* who used to return every spring and autumn to get money from the wreck or from some secret hiding place nearby. At all events, the fellow looked like a pirate, a genuine Billy Bones, and the family with whom he used to spend the night reported that he could not bear to remain in the room when the Bible or other religious book was read or family devotions performed. After retiring for the night it sounded as if he were entertaining a legion of infernals from the lower world in his room. He became frightfully noisy, profane, blasphemous, and quarrelsome. When he died, many gold pieces were found in a belt he had constantly worn.

Thoreau saw numerous wreckers at work along the Cape beaches, collecting flotsam and jetsam. He heard of one who had recently picked up twenty barrels of apples in good condition, probably part of a deckload thrown over in a storm. It was the custom of these Cape wreckers to place two crossed sticks on the property they had accumulated on the beach, to show others that it had been appropriated and must be let alone. Among the things which Thoreau himself found on the beach was a barnacle-covered bottle half buried in the wet sand. It was stoppled tight, and half-full of ale which he decanted on the sand. Finding the bottle gave him a chance for a bit of moralizing, but fortunately he did not repeat any of the nonsense from *Walden* about getting intoxicated on a glass of water.

The lower end of Chatham, which was once known as Scrabbletown, was a notorious nest of wreckers; nearly all the men in the place were engaged in the business, according to Joseph C. Lincoln, who tells an amusing story of a Scrabble-towner whom religion touched on the shoulder. This wrecker was preaching at a revival meeting one night when a small boy entered and, steering a course directly for the preacher, handed him a note. The missive, which was from the wrecker's partner, informed him that there was a vessel on the bar signalling for help. The lay preacher immediately requested the congregation to bow their heads for a few moments of silent prayer, and when all eyes were closed he tiptoed from the pulpit and left hurriedly for the beach by the back door.

A Provincetown character called Old John was among those who used to frequent the beach when the wind blew strongly, in the hope of finding something cast up by the sea on which he could make a dollar. One cold, starlit night, when it was blowing hard and the sand was frozen stiff, Old John trudged over to the bay side to see what he could pick up. Although conditions of wind and tide were favorable for a good haul and Old John knew the best places to go, his first skirmish along the hard-packed sands yielded nothing. But Old

John had a fisherman's patience and knew that his luck might momentarily turn. So he began a lonely patrol of the shore, walking back and forth confidently hopeful. He kept this up until nearly midnight, but with such discouraging results that at last, weary and half-frozen, he reluctantly turned homeward.

In the lee of a sand hill he paused to light his pipe, but before he could get it going he was startled by a sepulchral groan and the appearance of a large dark object that crested the dune and came rapidly down the slope straight for him. It was too dark for him to see what it was, nor did he feel like lingering to find out. Dropping his pipe, Old John took to his heels, with the terrifying thing in full cry after him. He ran some distance across the dunes before he ventured to look back, when to his horror he discovered that the dark menace was gaining on him. At length, thoroughly winded and with all hope of reaching the safety of the town gone, he resolved to make a last-ditch stand. Drawing his clasp knife, he turned to face his attacker, but as he did so missed his footing and fell. With a loud groan the dark object charged down upon him. It passed a few feet from him, coming to a halt in a tangle of beach plum bushes fifty feet beyond. Scrambling to his feet, Old John, knife in hand, now took the offensive, but there was no struggle. On reaching the bushes, he found that the thing which had pursued him was an empty water barrel propelled by the wind across the sands. The groaning was caused by the wind blowing into the bung hole in the side. Shouldering the barrel, Old John took it home, and afterward liked to relate his adventure and exhibit the barrel which had chased him across the sands.

The stranding of a vessel often gave work to the people of the Cape who salvaged the cargo for the owners or underwriters. But even then it seems to have been understood that those engaged in this work would help themselves. If the cargo was sugar, coffee, or similar commodity, pilfering was easy. The men would bring their dinners in the largest possible containers short of a barrel—"What big appetites you have, gentlemen!"—and fill them before going home. Others poured sugar into their trousers tied at the knees. One ingenious wrecker had a bag under his clothing which hung down in front on tapes from his shoulders. He was a thin enough looking fellow when he came to work, but by the end of the day he had developed a prodigious potbelly. A wrecker in such a case who failed to smuggle a barrel of sugar for himself didn't know his business.

There were so many wrecks around Cape Cod that a queer trade called anchor-dragging sprang up and flourished for many years. The anchor-draggers fished with grappling hooks and lines for lost anchors and other kinds of marine hardware from sunken vessels, such as ship's bells, wire rope, chains, blocks, and brass and other metal fittings. Most of the wreck material retrieved from the depths was sold by the pound as junk. On some shoals, where many vessels had gone down, it used to be said there were so many old anchors and other pieces of ironmongery lying around that the compasses of vessels that ventured near were affected. This branch of the wrecker's calling was centered largely in South Yarmouth, says Henry C. Kittredge in his *Mooncussers of Cape Cod*, the anchor-draggers finding the waters off that port a particularly good field for their combing operations.

Unpleasant scenes were enacted on the beach near Provincetown when the Italian bark *Giovanni* was wrecked March 4, 1875. She was eighty-one days out of Palermo, with a cargo of wine and fruit. She had experienced bad weather all the way and off the Massachusetts coast ran into a gale accompanied by snow that cut down the visibility worse than fog. Her frozen canvas was torn to shreds and the helpless craft was driven ashore at low water two and a half miles east of the Peaked Hill Life Saving Station. Her plight was discovered when the snow, settling for a moment as in a glass ball, brought her to view; however, there was nothing those on shore could do to help her crew.

A lifeboat was dragged through deep snow to the

scene, but it could not be launched through the heavy seas that were running. Huge chunks of drift ice added to the danger and hastened the destruction of the ship. Attempts were made to get a line to her with the wreck gun, without success, though the lifesavers tried until all their ammunition was used up.

A fire was built on the beach and maintained through the night. In the morning the ship was still there, but it was apparent the end was at hand. The crew, which had taken to the rigging, now worked their way out on the foreyard arm and one by one dropped into the sea. Only the ship's steward reached the beach alive. He clung to a plank and a young man of Provincetown with a strong rope tied round his waist dashed into the surf and rescued him. One man who was supposed to have been the captain remained afloat for forty-five minutes, but he could make no progress shoreward against the current and undertow. Thirteen died in the disaster. Soon after the crew abandoned her, the *Giovanni* went to pieces, portions of the wreckage and cargo being washed up for miles along the shore. As long as the wine lasted the beach was not a safe place for anyone. Men and boys reeled about hideously intoxicated, or lay dead drunk in the snow. "Men wandered up and down in the bitter cold, intent upon robbery and violence. One or more of these beach pirates were found dead, the victims of their own debauch."

A warm, spring-like day in February used to bring to the minds of Cape Cod folk the pleasant, almost summery Sunday of February 21, 1802, which was unexpectedly followed by one of the worst storms in the annals of the region and the wrecking of three proud, richly-laden East Indiamen from Salem. These splendid, full-rigged ships were the *Ulysses,* the *Brutus,* and the *Volusia,* commanded, respectively, by Captain James Cook, Captain William Brown, and Captain Samuel Cook. They had sailed together from Salem that Sunday morning, and the following day came ashore very near each other on the nether Cape.

The winter had been an unusually mild one and people were looking forward to an early spring when on the day before Washington's Birthday the weather suddenly changed. The day began mildly enough, but the wind shifted and that evening saw the beginning of a terrific northeast storm of snow, sleet, and wind, accompanied by intense cold, that lasted almost a week. The Massachusetts coast was littered with wrecks, at least a score of vessels being cast ashore, with the loss of numerous lives. Cape Cod, as usual, was the scene of the worst of these disasters.

When the three East Indiamen left Salem, two of them, the *Ulysses* and the *Brutus,* were bound for

Bordeaux, the *Volusia* for a Mediterranean port. It was a quiet day on the water, with a light south-easterly breeze and the ships were standing on an east northeast course. They made little progress during the afternoon and by sundown were only about ten miles southeast of Thatcher Island Light at Cape Ann. Shortly after this the weather shut down. It began to snow and otherwise look extremely threatening. The ships were too near the coast for comfort, so late in the evening they drew close together for a consultation of their captains. The question was whether they should run for home to await more favorable weather, or get out to sea as speedily as possible. Deciding on the latter course, they crowded on more canvas. It now began to snow in deadly earnest, and about midnight the wind backed around to the northeast and blew strongly. At half past two in the morning Captain Samuel Cook of the *Volusia*, disliking the outlook, decided to return to Salem, but in the darkness and snow he could not see the others to tell them of his change of plan.

The storm increased so rapidly in blinding fury it was soon apparent to the commander of the *Volusia* that it would be impossible to make Salem Harbor. His main hope now seemed to be to run before the wind and try to keep the ship off the shore. Under reefed topsails they succeeded in doing this until late in the morning. At eleven o'clock land was seen to leeward. It was the land they dreaded most—Cape Cod. Their only chance now lay in weathering the Cape and making Provincetown Harbor. But as they tacked, the foretopsail sheet parted, and the wind tore the sail to ribbons. Almost simultaneously the slings of the fore-yard were carried away, which brought that spar crashing to the deck, making it impossible to use the headsails. All hope of reaching Provincetown now vanished. It could be only a matter of minutes before they would be among the breakers. Actually, it was ten minutes before the ship struck the outer bar a mile from shore near the Peaked Hills off Truro. Anticipating this, the crew had cut away the mizzenmast, and now went to work on the mainmast, which soon went by the board too. Fortunately, the ship did not linger long on the outer bar, but beat over it, and was driven close to the land. In this position the crew waited until low tide that afternoon, when, with the help of the inhabitants who had gathered on the beach, all hands reached shore safely. Eventually the *Volusia* and part of her cargo were salvaged in badly damaged condition.

As for the *Ulysses* and the *Brutus*, they continued on their seaward course after the *Volusia* left them, but about half past three in the morning the two captains spoke to each other and decided that their best course lay in tacking to the north northwest until day, and then trying to run out the south channel. Accordingly, they changed their course, continuing on the new one until six o'clock, when the *Brutus* headed southeast, while the *Ulysses* steered for Cape Ann.

The *Ulysses* was held to the Cape Ann course until eight o'clock. She was then brought about and headed out of Massachusetts Bay, carrying all the canvas she could stagger under. This had to be reduced during the afternoon because of the increased intensity of the gale. Her reefed foresail and mizzen topsails were all she could carry. Captain Cook tacked to the westward when the Highlands of Cape Cod were seen at five o'clock, but there was then little expectation that the *Ulysses* could weather the Cape. Yet she managed to keep off the shoals until ten o'clock that night, when she struck the outer bar about a mile from the place where the *Volusia* had hit that morning. The bowsprit and foremast were torn away, quickly followed by the main- and mizzenmasts and everything on deck, including the ship's boats. Wind and waves made a clean sweep of her. The crew fled to the cabin, believing their last minutes were at hand. But as in the case of the *Volusia*, the *Ulysses* did not remain long on the outer bar, huge waves heaving her over and driving her toward the beach. Her position, however, was not near enough for the crew to get ashore, and to add to the terror of the situation, the ship had bilged on the bar and was filling. Along toward morning, when the water had risen above the cabin floor, the tide reached its lowest point, leaving the hull stranded so close inshore that the crew had no difficulty in landing. Some Provincetown people were on hand to assist them. A portion of the damaged cargo was salvaged, but the ship was a total loss.

The *Brutus* met the same fate as the other two ships, struggling gallantly all day to weather the tempest, only to be overwhelmed at last on the sands of Cape Cod. Crowding on all possible sail when she parted company with the *Ulysses* early Monday morning, the *Brutus* stood to the south-eastward, but during the day gradually lost ground as she was slowly beaten shoreward. So fierce was the violence of the wind that one of the crew, a Salem youth named Andrew Herron, was blown from the yard while trying to reef the foresail and instantly killed by the fall. The *Brutus* struck on the outer bar at eight o'clock that night about two miles from Highland Light, not far from where her sister ships were wrecked. Here she remained for some time, taking a terrible pounding, until the greater part of her cargo had been jettisoned; thus lightened, she was lifted over by the waves and grounded on the inner shoals close to shore. The main- and mizzenmasts were cut away to lighten her further, but this had no sooner been accomplished than it was found the ship was breaking in two. The crew had to abandon her at once, but how to get ashore through the surf was a problem. Luckily, the mainmast had fallen toward the land and by crawling along this as far as it would take them, the crew, under the leadership of Captain Brown, succeeded in getting ashore. Only one man failed, George Pierce of Marblehead, who was swept away and drowned as he tried to land.

Their troubles, however, were not over when they reached the shore. To be wrecked on a desolate beach at night during a fierce storm, with no sign of a human habitation anywhere, is not a happy situation to be in, especially in sub-zero weather. But that was the position in which the crew of the *Brutus* found themselves. Wet and perishing with the cold, they could not remain on the beach. They had to find shelter quickly. It was decided that they would stay together and cross to the bay side of the Cape in search of protection. So they started across the dunes, trudging painfully through the deep snow, hoping momentarily to discover a house or barn.

Captain Brown, who was coatless, was the first to succumb. The march proved too exhausting for him, and though Thomas Ruee, the first mate, and others helped him, they could not save the captain. He collapsed and died soon after they reached the western side of the Cape between Provincetown and

Truro. Had their course across the Cape been slightly to the right or to the left they would have struck Provincetown or Truro. It was now midnight; the party, hopelessly lost, continued to wander among the dunes. As the night wore on, the band gradually diminished. First one and then another dropped from exhaustion and quietly froze to death in the snow. At length, about four o'clock in the morning, when only five were left, they saw a lighthouse. Stumbling in that direction, they came to a house, where they were mercifully received and everything possible was done for them.

An immediate search was made for those who had fallen in the snow, but all were beyond help. One seaman, Benjamin Ober of Manchester, was found alive after being buried in the sand and snow for thirty-six hours. People had passed near him many times, but he had been too weak to attract their attention. Finally, a boy saw him raise his hand through the snow. He was taken to the nearest house, but it was too late. He died soon after. Of the crew of fourteen officers and men on the *Brutus,* nine, including three Negroes, lost their lives. The captain was buried in Provincetown, the others in Truro.

Blunt, in his *Coast Pilot,* states that the Humane Society had built a hut as a refuge for shipwrecked mariners a few rods from the place where the crew of the *Brutus* landed, but it was improperly constructed and placed where no beach grass grew. The strong winds blew the sand from the foundation and the weight of the chimney brought the whole structure to the ground. This was in January 1802, only a few weeks before the wreck of the *Brutus*. It was felt that had it remained, the entire crew probably would have been saved.

After a severe easterly storm in 1880, the skeleton of a man was found who was thought to have perished with the *Brutus*. It came to light when part of the bank on which the wreck of the ship had rested was washed away. With the skeleton there were some silver coins and a watch that had stopped at two o'clock. These relics had been buried in the sand for seventy-eight years.

Wrecks long hidden have frequently come to light. Perhaps the most remarkable for length of interment was the discovery in 1863 of the remains of a vessel at Nauset Beach. Remnants of the hull were discovered embedded in the mud of a meadow near the water. Removed and examined, they were seen to be those of a ship of very ancient construction, believed to have been buried more than two centuries. Everything pointed to the remains being those of the *Sparrow Hawk*, mentioned by Bradford as having been cast ashore in 1626.

From the point of view of lives lost, one of the worst sea disasters on the New England coast was the wreck of the steamer *Portland* off the tip of

Cape Cod late in November, 1898. Out of one hundred and thirty-seven passengers and a crew of one hundred men, there was not a single survivor. What actually happened is still a mystery, but Fred Erving Dayton, the historian of steamboating, has gathered all the known facts and from these has made certain deductions which are probably as near the truth as we are likely to get.

The *Portland* was a wooden side-wheeler of 2,283 tons built in 1890 expressly for the passenger service between Boston and Maine. She had two stacks, measured 291 feet in length, with a beam of 42 feet, except amidships over the paddle-wheel guards where she was 68 feet wide, and she had a hold depth of 15½ feet. Like similar broadly-built side-wheelers, the *Portland* was very steady, but she was a shoal-draft, fair-weather ship, not intended to withstand severe storms. If the weather looked threatening, she was held in port, and if conditions became bad while she was out, she took refuge in the nearest harbor. At no time during her runs along the coast was she very far from a safe haven, but her captain had to be a good judge of the weather and know when to run for it.

The *Portland* sailed from India Wharf, Boston, at 7 o'clock Saturday night, November 26, on her regular run to Portland, Maine. At the time there was a light easterly wind and an overcast sky, but nothing to indicate that an unusually bad storm was brewing. The *Portland* had a speed of twelve knots an hour and generally covered the run between Boston and Portland in eight hours more or less, depending on the weather. Shortly after passing Deer Island Light at 7:20, the *Portland* ran into a snowstorm. She came out of this and at 9:30 was sighted by the fishing schooner *Maude S.* only a mile or two from the twin lights of Cape Ann. This was the last time she was seen afloat.

At the government investigation, in which it was sought to fix the blame on the captain of the *Portland*, the skipper of the *Maude S.* testified that at the time he saw the *Portland* he did not consider the captain was taking any chance in continuing to Portland. He had himself thought of keeping on to Boston, but had decided to put into Gloucester. Whether or not the schooner could have reached Boston is a question, as the storm was then advancing along the coast at a lively rate, drawing in northeasterly winds that were rapidly developing gale strength. By midnight, or soon after, it was blowing a hurricane, with the wind sometimes reaching ninety miles an hour. It was no weather for the *Portland* to be out in. She could make no progress in a storm of such intensity. But the rest of that night and all through the following day she made a brave fight for life. It must have been a period of the utmost terror for those on board.

The first news of the *Portland's* fate came at 7:30

Sunday evening when a surfman of the Race Point Life Saving Station at the end of the Cape, who had been patrolling the beach to the eastward, reported masses of wreckage coming ashore about three miles from the station. The bulk of it washed up on the beach in less than an hour, though pieces continued coming in for days afterward. Very few bodies were recovered, not more than a dozen or so being cast up by the sea during the next two weeks. Most of these were found near Highland Light, the rest along the shore as far south as Chatham.

Examining the evidence in the case, Mr. Dayton concludes that the *Portland* lasted until about six o'clock Sunday night. He thought that after she had last been seen by the *Maude S.* near Gloucester she continued on her course until shortly after midnight, when she was well along the coast between Cape Ann and Cape Elizabeth. The violence of the storm then made it impossible for her to proceed any farther. Instead of making headway, she was slowly but steadily driven southward across the bay, drawing on her last reserves of coal to keep her head up. He thought she held together until six o'clock, because if she had gone to pieces Sunday morning, her timbers would have been swept into the bay by the northeast wind, and if in the afternoon, the strong tide setting into the bay would have done the same thing. But her wreckage coming ashore where it did showed she either foundered or was smashed to pieces near Peaked Hill Bar off the northern end of the Cape. When she perished it didn't take her remains long to come piling in on the sands.

An interesting footnote to the *Portland* disaster was added during the early part of 1899. The schooner *Maude S.*, while fishing on the Stellwagon Bank off the extremity of the Cape, recovered some stateroom fixtures which had belonged to the *Portland*. It was the loss of this ship that did much to destroy public confidence in the old side-wheelers, and the sound of their spanking paddles along the New England coast soon died away.

They still have shipwrecks on Cape Cod, but not so many as in the old days. The great stream of coastwise sailing vessels is a thing of the past, and modern aids to navigation have robbed the sea of many of its former perils. Many ships and tugs with tows which formerly had to round the Cape can now use the Cape Cod Canal. The canal not only makes it possible to avoid the outside run along the exposed easterly side of the Cape, but shortens the distance between New York and Boston by nearly seventy miles. The distance between the dredged entrance to the canal off Wings Neck Lighthouse in Buzzards Bay to the end of the 3,000-foot stone breakwater protecting the Cape Cod Bay entrance is eleven and a half miles. The canal proper is eight miles long, five hundred feet wide, and can be used by vessels up to twenty-eight foot draft. Tidal currents in the canal under ordinary conditions have a velocity of about three and a half knots. Transit of the waterway is made alternately by eastbound and westbound traffic. The canal is owned and operated by the United States government and no tolls are charged.

The advantages of a canal cutting through the collar of the Cape were apparent even to the Pilgrims, who, as already related, established a trading house on the neck of the Cape within a few years of the founding of Plymouth. By order of the General Court of Massachusetts the feasibility of building a canal was explored in 1697. General Henry Knox, our first Secretary of War, was also interested in a canal here for military reasons, but a century more passed before anything was done, and when the task was at length undertaken it was as a private rather than a governmental enterprise.

Early in the present century August Belmont decided to try his hand at building the long-projected canal. Work was begun in 1909 and the canal was opened in 1914. Belmont spent $17,000,000 on it. In 1926, the United States government bought it for $11,500,000, but this was only the beginning. The two highway bridges and the railroad bridge spanning the canal were constructed at a cost of $5,000,000, and improvements to the canal and its approaches have been made to the tune of many more millions. But it is an important waterway through which a great deal of shipping passes with far more safety and dispatch than if it were forced to take the long outside route.

Cape Cod, with its numerous lighthouses and lighted buoys, has a well-illuminated coast, but for more than half of its civilized life it was a dark and dangerous place without any system of beaconage. The first lighthouse was Cape Cod Light, or Highland Light, as it is now called. Established in 1798 on the highlands on the northeast side of the Cape, it was rebuilt in 1857. It was followed in 1808 by the lighthouse at Chatham, and in 1816 by Race Point Light on the northwest point of the Cape, both of which have since been rebuilt. Others were added from time to time.

We are so in the habit of thinking of our lighthouse service in its present enlightened and efficient state, it is difficult to realize that until the middle of the nineteenth century it was probably the worst on the civilized globe. One man delivered all the supplies, made whatever repairs and changes he chose, and had the supervision of things largely centered in his hands, with the result that there was little oversight of the service. He acted without any instructions from anybody, as did also the keepers, who complained about the quality of everything—the oil, the polish, the frames. One gets an inkling of all this by reading Thoreau's account of his stay at Highland Light. Things drifted along unsatisfactorily for years—through most of the sailing-ship era, in fact—until at length the head of the Lighthouse Board woke up and became very, very angry when he learned the true state of affairs. There was a turn for the better.

With a diminishing number of wrecks to batten on, the old-time mooncussing trade fell on evil days.

WHERE do whales go in their spare time?
Formerly great numbers of them sported and
played around Cape Cod as lightheartedly as summer people do today, but as the inhabitants of the
Cape were wont to pursue and attack them, the
creatures wisely withdrew, giving the place a wider
and wider berth, until their nursery is now said to
be in the remote South Atlantic, well off the normal
shipping routes. A motor freighter which traversed

this region during the war reported seeing thousands of whales four hundred miles east of Tristan da Cunha, feeding in family groups on sea anemones. After proceeding for a hundred miles through this sea of whales, there were no more sea anemones and the whales were no longer seen. Whales still appear occasionally off Cape Cod, but seldom in schools any more.

The Pilgrims were greatly impressed by the number they saw at Provincetown during the weeks the *Mayflower* lay at anchor in the harbor after the long Atlantic crossing. "And every day," Mourt says in his *Relation*, "we saw whales playing hard by us, of which in that place, if we had instruments and means to take them, we might have made a very rich return; which, to our great grief, we wanted. Our master, and his mate, and others experienced in fishing, professed we might have made three or four thousand pounds' worth of oil. They preferred it to Greenland whale-fishing, and purpose the next winter to fish for whale here."

Whaling in New England began at Truro and Wellfleet long before Nantucket, Martha's Vineyard, and New Bedford took to it. It was, indeed, a Cape man, Ichabod Paddock, who was invited to instruct the Nantucketers in the art of killing whales in boats from the shore. This professional harpooner was a native of Yarmouth, but was living in Truro when in 1690 the call came from Nantucket.

Later, another Truro man, Captain Jesse Holbrook, who on one voyage speared no fewer than fifty-four sperm whales, became an instructor in a whaling school maintained by a private company in London, where he taught whaling for twelve years. Captain Holbrook belonged to the famous Truro whaling gang known as the Seed Corners, a name derived from the fact that Truro was the place where the Pilgrims had found the hidden store of seed corn which stood them in such good stead their first year at Plymouth.

Lookouts were maintained at Whale House Hill and other places along the Truro shore. When a whale was sighted the watcher cried, "Towner!" This was then the view halloo or tallyho of the whale hunters, which later became "There she blows!" It was an Indian word meaning the whale has been seen twice. It is said that the shouts of the leather-lunged lookouts, which were picked up and repeated, could be heard for two miles.

Massachusetts Bay was a favorite resort of whales, because for centuries the creatures had been largely undisturbed there, and the food was plentiful and good. The gigantic arm of the Cape gathered in vast shoals of the kind of fishes on which the whales liked to feed. In pursuing these, the whales sometimes got into shallow water and were stranded on the beach by the ebbing tide, where they fell an easy prey to the Indians. These were the so-called drift whales, about which there was a great deal of controversy in the old days. Even the government claimed a share. There is a letter written by a colonial secretary suggesting to the Cape towns that a hogshead of oil from each drift whale delivered without charge at Boston would be satisfactory to the provincial authorities; this was later raised to two barrels. Barnstable County also insisted on a barrel. The town of Sandwich sold the right to all drift whales to a group of three men for the flat sum of sixteen pounds per whale, the person who found the whale being entitled to twenty shillings. When only part of a whale came ashore, which sometimes happened, the hope was keen that it would be the head end rather than the tail end, for a whale's tongue could yield as much as twenty or twenty-five barrels of oil.

In some places, shares in whales were allotted to the minister and schoolmaster. In 1662, the town of Eastham agreed that a part of every whale washed up on the shore should be appropriated to the maintenance of the ministry. Thoreau liked the idea of thus leaving the support of the clergy to Providence. He pictured the ministers sitting on the heights in every storm, anxiously watching the shore to see if a whale were having the breath of life beaten out of him by the tempest and being dragged in over the bars. "For my part," he said, "if I were a minister, I would rather trust to the bowels of the billows, on the back side of Cape Cod, to cast up a whale for me, than to the generosity of many a country parish that I know."

Chasing whales from the shore in open boats was not only part of the struggle for existence on the Cape, but an adventure and a sport as well. It was a picturesque form of hunting which created intense excitement, and the cry spreading through a community that there were whales in the offing stirred everyone. Even the women went to watch the struggle of the men in the boats with the great ocean beasts. In some places whale hunting was a communal affair. Chatham had a whaleboat held by the citizens on shares.

After the whales had pretty much left the seacoast of New England, two Truro skippers, Captain David Smith and Captain Gamaliel Collins, were the first to go whaling to the Falkland Islands. This was done in 1774 at the suggestion of Admiral Montague of the Royal Navy, or "Mad" Montague, as he was called. It was good advice, as both ventures proved immensely successful. At that time there were nearly forty whalers owned in various Cape Cod ports.

It was the custom of those who pursued whales in the coastal waters of the Cape to register the marks on their lances with the local town officials, as they registered their cattle marks. This was done so that when a whale which had been harpooned drifted ashore the person who had killed it could claim the whale as his property. Thus we find the following note in the Truro records:

"Joshua Atwood's lance that he hath made on purpose to kill finbacks with a three-square head marked W. R.

> "John Snow, *Town Clerk*.
> "*Received Feby.*, 1719-20."

A whale swimming in the sea is not property, and belongs to no one until there is some act of appropriation. In the case of wild creatures generally the animal must be reduced to the actual possession and control of the person claiming ownership. But very early in the history of American whaling the usage was established that the iron holds the whale. The custom was finally challenged in a dispute that arose over a dead whale found on the sands of Cape Cod. This was the case of Ghen *v.* Rich (8 Federal Rep. 159), decided in 1881. Because it involved a marine matter, the case was tried in the Federal Court. The proceedings, which were begun by an admiralty complaint or libel, were for the purpose of recovering the value of a finback whale. The libellant lived in Provincetown, the respondent in Wellfleet. The facts, as they appeared at the hearing, were summarized as follows in the decision of District Judge Nelson:

"In the early spring months the easterly part of Massachusetts Bay is frequented by the species of whale known as the finback whale. Fishermen from Provincetown pursue them in open boats from the shore and shoot them with bomb-lances fired from guns made expressly for the purpose. When killed they sink at once to the bottom, but in the course of from one to three days they rise and float on the surface. Some of them are picked up by vessels and towed into Provincetown. Some float ashore at high water and are left stranded on the beach as the tide recedes. Others float out to sea and are never recovered. The person who finds them on the beach usually sends word to Provincetown and the owner comes to the spot and removes the blubber. The finder usually receives a small salvage for his services. Try-works are established at Provincetown for trying out the oil. The business is of considerable extent, but since it requires skill and experience, as well as some outlay of capital, and is attended with great exposure and hardship, few persons engage in it. The average yield of oil is about twenty barrels to a whale. It swims with great swiftness, and for that reason cannot be taken by the harpoon and line. Each boat's crew engaged in the business has its peculiar mark or device on its lances, and in this way it is known by whom the whale was killed.

"The usage on Cape Cod, for many years," Judge

Nelson continues, "has been that the person who kills a whale in the manner and under the circumstances described, owns it, and this right has never been disputed until this case. The libellant has been engaged in this business for ten years past. On the morning of April 9, 1880, in Massachusetts Bay, near the end of Cape Cod, he shot and instantly killed with a bomb-lance the whale in question. It sank immediately, and on the morning of the 12th was found stranded on the beach in Brewster, within the ebb and flow of the tide, by one Ellis, seventeen miles from the spot where it was killed. Instead of sending word to Provincetown, as is customary, Ellis advertised the whale for sale at auction, and sold it to the respondent, who stripped off the blubber and tried out the oil. The libellant heard of the finding of the whale on the 15th, and immediately sent one of his boat's crew to the place and claimed it. Neither the respondent nor Ellis knew the whale had been killed by the libellant, but they knew or might have known, if they had wished, that it had been shot and killed with a bomb-lance, by some person engaged in this species of business."

Title to the whale was claimed, under the usage mentioned, by the Provincetown man who killed it, while the Wellfleet purchaser insisted that this usage was invalid. The court held that the custom proved in the case that the iron holds the whale was reasonable and valid. It had been recognized and acquiesced in for many years. It required in the first taker the only act of appropriation possible in the nature of the case. Unless the usage was sustained, this branch of the industry would necessarily cease, for no person would enage in it if the fruits of his labor could be appropriated by any chance finder. The measure of damages was the market value of the oil obtained from the whale, less the cost of trying it out and preparing it for the market, with interest on the amount so ascertained from the date of the conversion, which in the case of Ghen *v.* Rich was found to be seventy-one dollars and some odd cents.

For many years the Cape was haunted by a whistling whale which made lonesome sounds in the night. The mystery was solved when it was caught—a harpoon was embedded in its blowpipes, a New Bedford lance which had been plunged into the monster fourteen years before. After so long a period it could hardly be said that the iron held the whale.

One of the largest finbacks ever killed at Provincetown was taken by Captain Joshua S. Nickerson in the whaling schooner *A. B. Nickerson.* This leviathan was sixty-five feet four inches in length, with a girth of thirty-seven feet. It measured fourteen feet six inches across the tail and had ten-foot flukes. Its lower jaw was eleven feet long, the capacity of its mouth when closed thirty barrels.

Its estimated weight was one hundred and thirty-six tons. Some enterprising men from Chicago bought the dead whale, loaded it on special railroad cars, and exhibited it through the Middle West until decomposition kept people away. A Cape Codder, Captain Newton P. West, acted as lecturer.

Whalemen, hoping to strike it rich, were forever on the lookout for ambergris. This is a curious substance disgorged by sperm whales, and is worth hundreds of dollars a pound because of its value as a fixative of the scent in perfume. It is usually found floating in tropical waters, in pieces weighing fifteen or twenty pounds. The crew of the schooner *Montezuma* of Provincetown, however, while cutting into a sperm whale which they had killed on the Mosquito Coast, struck a hard substance like pumice stone that proved to be a large piece of ambergris estimated to weigh over one hundred pounds. The wind was blowing hard at the time and a heavy sea running. In their haste to get the precious stuff aboard, it was improperly secured, and to the dismay of the crew, it slipped from the slings while being hoisted to the deck, and plunged into the sea between the whale and the vessel, and sank in sixty fathoms of water, a loss to the Cape Codders of more than $25,000.

One reads of the great rewards of whaling, but actually the rank and file engaged in this extremely hazardous adventure were not well rewarded.

There were times, of course, when it paid handsomely, and it was undoubtedly the lure of prosperous voyages that attracted many men to the hunt; but nine times out of ten a man came home indebted to the ship's owner. Before embarking, a whaleman had to have an outfit of clothes and other necessaries which were charged to him at high prices. While the daily subsistence of his family during his absence depended almost entirely on fish taken with a line or shellfish raked out of the sand, his wife had to have credit at a store for clothing and staples. Not oftener than once in a decade was his share in a voyage large enough to wipe out his indebtedness to the ship owner. He had to go when called for the next voyage, or be jailed for debt; the new voyage meant a new outfit, more credit for his wife, and almost certainly a deeper sinking into debt. No wonder it was often necessary to go elsewhere for men to fill out the crews.

It was whaling that first brought the Portuguese to Provincetown more than a century ago, though Gaspard Cortereal, a "Portingale," was on the North American coast before any of the English navigators. Cabot merely sailed by, but the Portuguese landed. They introduced domestic animals to Sable Island thirty years before Gilbert came to Newfoundland. The Cape Cod whaleships used to put into the Azores and the Cape Verde Islands to recruit their crews, and it wasn't long before Provincetown had a Portuguese colony. Today, three-quarters of the permanent population of 4,000 are Portuguese, the rest mostly old Cape Cod stock. These Portuguese, who control the town politically, are made up of "Azoreans" from the Azores, "Lisbons" from Portugal proper, and a sprinkling of black "Bravas," who came originally from the Cape Verde Islands. The old Cape Cod expression for any meeting at which everyone talks and nobody listens is a "Portuguese parliament."

Samuel Adams Drake, who visited Provincetown in 1875, was impressed by the dark-skinned Portuguese women. "In my rambles," he said, "I met with a band of them returning from the swamp region back of the town. They looked gypsylike with their swarthy faces and gleaming eyes. The younger women had clear olive complexions, black eyes, and the elongated Madonna faces of their race; the older ones were grisly and witchlike, with shriveled bodies and wrinkled faces. All of them bore bundles of faggots on their heads that our tender women would have sunk under, yet they did not seem in the least to mind them. They chattered merrily as they passed me, and I watched them until out of sight; for, picturesque objects anywhere, here they were doubly so. They all had gaudy handkerchiefs tied about their heads, and shawls worn sashwise, and knotted at the hip, the bright bits of warm color contrasting kindly with the dead white sand. There were shapely figures among them."

At least two Provincetowners have had the exciting experience of riding through the sea on a whale's back. Years ago, while humpback whaling on the Spanish Main, a boat's crew from a Provincetown vessel struck one of the creatures which promptly retaliated by upsetting the boat and scattering the crew. One of the men landed on the slippery back of the whale near the harpoon which was sticking up in the whale's flesh. Grabbing this support, he held on as the whale rushed off through the water at top speed. After going some distance dragging the rope attached to the harpoon, the whale turned and came charging back toward the vessel. As the whale passed near a whaleboat engaged in rescuing the men clinging to the capsized boat, the man on the whale's back jumped off and swam to it, carrying the harpoon line still fast to the whale. The second boat's crew then proceeded to capture the beast.

On June 27, 1948, two Provincetown fishermen, Frank Cabral, Jr., aged seventeen, and his father, claimed that they were attacked by a whale while they were out in separate dories tending their gang of lobster traps off Race Point. The whale swam directly for the elder Cabral's dory but submerged before striking it and came up under the son's boat. Young Cabral was spilled out onto the whale's back.

There was no harpoon for him to cling to, but he somehow managed to stay on as the monster headed out to sea. The father started in pursuit of his son and the whale, but before he could get near them the whale decided to sound. As he slowed down, the youth on his back abandoned his mount, striking out for his own dory, which fortunately had not been overturned. The whale, in hitting the boat, had splintered a hole in it and had taken a gouge out of its own back. The hole and a piece of blubber were shown in confirmation of the story.

How fast does a whale rider travel? It is difficult to say, except that it is at a very speedy pace. A whale can glide through the water with the greatest of ease at twelve miles an hour. Maddened by a harpoon thrust, it can do twenty-five, which is faster than most ocean shipping.

Another Provincetown person, an experienced whaleman named Franklin Atkins, had an even more sensational experience with a whale than riding on its back. While pursuing whales off the West Indies he was in a boat that attacked a huge sperm whale. Harpooned, the whale smashed the boat with its flukes, and tossed it into the air, so that everybody was thrown out. The whale happened to have its mouth open and Atkins fell into it. He was quite badly wounded from landing on the monster's teeth, but he managed to get out before the great jaws closed, and succeeded in reaching the wreckage of the whaleboat, to which he clung until rescued. At-kins, who bore the scars of the whale's teeth on his back and side the rest of his life, used to say that he and Jonah were the only two persons who had been in a whale's mouth and come out alive.

Narrow escapes were common enough, and so were fatalities. One Cape Cod whaleman, who lost his life when a whale stove in his boat, was brought home in a barrel of rum. Besides the losses resulting from encounters with whales, there were those caused by the perils of the sea. There are many instances of whale ships vanishing, without a word as to their fate, not even a bottled message, ever being received.

The whaling brig *Ardent* with a crew of fourteen men was wrecked by a hurricane in September, 1823, while homeward bound after a successful cruise. The storm knocked her on her beam-ends, sweeping three men overboard and snapping off the masts close to the deck. Fortunately, the ship righted, but only a small portion of the after end remained above water. On this the surviving members of the crew took refuge. They could not get into the cabin for provisions and were without water. They were on the wreck twenty-six days, with only a few barnacles and an occasional small fish to eat, and a scanty supply of water secured during rain squalls. Six men died before rescue, and only four survived of those who were rescued by a British packet bound for Falmouth, England.

Yet against such tragedies one may set the many Cape Codders who spent practically all their lives at sea without mishap. John Young of Wellfleet was one of these; he was eighty-five when he died, and had engaged in whaling for fifty years.

It is perhaps worth noting that Herman Melville, author of the whaling classic, *Moby Dick*, married the daughter of a native of Cape Cod—Chief Justice Lemuel Shaw of the Massachusetts Supreme Court, a Barnstable man and one of the greatest jurists America has produced. Shaw's first fiancée was Nancy Melville, the writer's aunt, who died before Shaw could marry her. *Moby Dick* contains the best literary portrait of a Cape Cod whaleman— Stubb, the second mate of the *Pequod*, who loved to eat whalesteak cut from the small. "Hold the steak in one hand, and show a live coal to it with the other," he told the cook. Stubb's short, black pipe was one of the features of his face. He had a row of pipes ready loaded in a rack above his berth, and whenever he turned in he smoked them all in succession, then reloaded them to be in readiness when he turned out.

"He was a native of Cape Cod," says Melville; "and hence, according to local usage, was called a Cape-Cod-man. A happy-go-lucky; neither craven nor valiant; taking perils as they came with an in-

different air; and while engaged in the most im-
minent crisis of the chase, toiling away, calm and
collected as a journeyman joiner engaged for the
year. Good-humored, easy, and careless, he presided
over his whaleboat as if the most deadly encounter
were but a dinner, and his crew all invited guests.
He was as particular about the comfortable arrange-
ment of his part of the boat, as an old stagecoach
driver is about the snugness of his box. When close
to the whale, in the very death-lock of the fight, he
handled his unpitying lance coolly and offhandedly,
as a whistling tinker his hammer. He would hum
over his old rigadig tunes while flank and flank with
the most exasperated monster. Long usage had, for
this Stubb, converted the jaws of death into an easy
chair."

There was always great sport and excitement
when a school of pocket-size whales, called blackfish, ventured too near land and permitted themselves to be driven ashore and slaughtered.
Hundreds were often taken in a single drive, richly
rewarding the hunters. A vivid eyewitness account
of one of these drives seventy-five years ago gives
an excellent idea of what it was like.

"When the school were discovered near the
shore, the fishermen getting outside of them in
their dories, by halooing, sounding horns, and
other noises, drove them, like frightened sheep,
toward the beach. As soon as the hunters were in

shoal water they left their boats, and jumped overboard, urging the silly fish on by outcries, splashing
the water, and blows. Men, and even boys, waded
boldly up to a fish, and led him ashore by a fin; or,
if inclined to show fight, put their knives into him.
They cuffed them, pricked them onward, filling the
air with shouts, or with peals of laughter, as some
pursuer, more eager than prudent, lost his footing,
and became for the moment a fish. All this time
the blackfish were nearing the shore, uttering
sounds closely resembling groanings and lamenta-
tions. The calves kept close to the old ones. 'Squeal-
ing,' as one of the captors told me, 'like young pigs.'
It was great sport, not wholly free from danger, for
the fish can strike a powerful blow with its flukes;
and the air was filled with jets of water where they
had lashed it into foam."

Thoreau has described the blackfish he saw on
the beach at Truro in July, 1855. "When I came to
Great Hollow," he says, "I found a fisherman and
some boys on watch, and counted about thirty
blackfish, just killed, with many lance wounds, and
the water was more or less bloody around. They
were partly on shore and partly in the water, held
by a rope round their tails till the tide should leave
them. A boat had been somewhat stove by the tail
of one. They were a smooth shining black, like
India-rubber, and had remarkably simple and
lumpish forms for animated creatures, with a blunt

round snout or head, whale-like, and simple stiff-looking flippers. The largest was about fifteen feet long, but one or two were only five feet long, and still without teeth. The fisherman slashed one with his jackknife, to show me how thick the blubber was,—about three inches; and as I passed my finger through the cut it was covered thick with oil. The blubber looked like pork, and this man said that while they were trying it the boys would sometimes come round with a piece of bread in one hand, and take a piece of blubber in the other to eat with it, preferring it to pork scraps. He also cut into the flesh beneath, which was firm and red like beef, and he said that for his part, he preferred it when fresh to beef."

These Lilliputian whales yield about a barrel of oil apiece, and the refined oil, sometimes called porpoise-jaw oil, is used as a lubricant for watches and clocks. Practically the whole supply today is refined at New Bedford.

An incident during Kendall's visit to the Cape in 1807, while he was on his way from Truro to Provincetown by the bay route, is worth recalling, as it shows at what an early age the youth of Cape Cod began pursuing the monsters of the deep.

"At the distance of half a mile, on the sandy flat from which the sea was now fast retiring," says this visitor, "we discovered a boy and near him appeared to be a great fish. The solitariness of the boy and his smallness compared with the fish, formed a combination sufficiently remarkable to draw us to the spot; and we found our fisherman of about ten years' age, astride a porpoise upon the sand. Alone, and with a common table knife for his instrument, he was cutting the blubber from the ribs of the monster, a task which he performed in a very workmanlike manner. Upon inquiring, we learned that he alone had killed the fish. His employment in the morning had been attending his mother's cows; and from the hills on which he was, he had seen a shoal of porpoises enter the inlet. As the tide was ebbing and the shore flat, many of them were soon embarrassed by the want of sufficient water to move in; and he flattered himself that by leaving the cows and coming down to the beach, he might be able to make a prize. So going into the water as far as he dared, he selected one struggling to regain deep water. This fish he boldly caught, from time to time, by the tail, thereby increasing its difficulties, till at last the water running away left the porpoise upon the sand. He stayed by the fish till he was sure that escape was impossible; and then running home, a distance of a mile, procured a knife. Thus armed, he preceeded to wound and kill the fish—a task of some labor and danger; and according to his account, he had accomplished it by watching opportunities—alternately striking and retreating. My companion said it would yield ten gallons of oil, and give the little cowherd ten dollars for his exploit."

Few relics of the days of whaling are now extant, though occasionally one sees pieces of whalebone bleached white from years of exposure to the weather in the yards of old Cape houses. It was once fashionable to set up a pair of ribs or other parts of a whale's skeleton to form an arch over a gate. In the whalebone era, when corsets and horsewhips were made of the bone, a large portion of the profits of a voyage was derived from the sale of the bone, which brought several dollars a pound.

Log books of whaleships are still among the treasured possessions of some old Cape Cod families, but the ships themselves, of course, vanished long ago. The old leather-bound or canvas-covered logs make fascinating reading. It was usually the first mate's job to keep the log, which he wrote up from temporary notes made on a slate or slip of paper. The entries as a rule began with the direction of the wind and the ship's course. Any changes in these were carefully noted, and the ship's position, the latitude and longitude, given. A record was kept of such events as raising a sail, a gam with the crews of other ships met at sea, the boarding of a derelict, unusual phenomena observed, happenings on board outside the ordinary routine, and, of course, the pursuit and capture or escape of a whale.

In turning the pages of an old log book, it is easy

to spot the days on which a whale was killed, because the whale is pictured in silhouette. The picture was either drawn freehand or made with a small woodblock or die about two inches long, with a square white space in the center for noting the number of barrels of oil the whale yielded, at thirty gallons to the barrel. If the whale escaped, the tail only was drawn or printed. The silhouette showed the species of whale encountered. Thumbnail sketches of passing ships or the appearance of islands were also sometimes part of the record, and the entries usually closed with the words "So ends," which was the abbreviated form of "So ends another day by the grace of God."

One matter of record in the annals of Eastham presents a mystery which will probably never be solved. In 1660 a man in that town was fined one pound for "lying about a whale." One wonders what kind of whopper he told.

The discovery of oil in Pennsylvania in 1857 brought to a speedy close the fabled days of New England's whaling industry, which had begun two centuries before at Cape Cod.

THE first windmill in New England was built at Watertown, near Boston, in 1631. The Indians were afraid of windmills, imagining that the giant arms were turned by an evil spirit inside the mill, which bit the corn to pieces between its terrible teeth.

Windmills flourish where there is a scarcity of convenient water power, so it is not surprising to find that soon after the settlement of Cape Cod, mill towers began to punctuate the landscape. But if the

Cape was somewhat lacking in water power, particularly at the lower end, it had plenty of wind to drive the sails of its mills. Eventually it came to have more windmills than any other section of New England. These mills were the first pieces of machinery constructed in the country.

Before gristmills were established, the colonists had to use the primitive and tedious process of pounding corn by hand with a stone or wooden pestle in a mortar made of the hollow stump of a tree. This laborious method was sometimes lightened by suspending the heavy pestle from the top of a sapling bent over the mortar to make what was known as a sweep and mortar mill. Crude handmills, called quernes or quarnes, were also used, but there was nothing quite so effective for grinding corn as the stones of a watermill or windmill. Even today the ancient mills grind beautifully "live" meal, which the old-fashioned miller, farmer, and baker will tell you is better than that which is produced by speedy, modern mill machinery.

Less than a dozen old windmills remain on Cape Cod today, where once they were an outstanding feature of the countryside. They were conspicuous because they were built in exposed situations to catch the wind. A semicircle of three is mentioned in Blunt's *American Coast Pilot* for 1827 as a landmark for Chatham. The steepled meeting house at Brewster, with a windmill not far from it, was another prominent navigation aid. Truro had a number of windmills, at least one of which stood on the same high plateau as its two meeting houses. These structures formed a famous guide for mariners on the bay.

The tall tower of this Truro windmill, built early in the nineteenth century, was constructed of heavy Southern timber from a vessel wrecked on the ocean-side of the town. Oxen hauled the great beams to the Hill of Storms, and at the raising a wash barrel of grog was consumed. The long leg extending from the cap of the mill to the wheel on the ground, by which the sails were made to head into the wind, was the mast of a dismantled schooner, measuring nearly one hundred feet in length.

Shebnah Rich, the bearded historian of Truro (a picture of him is the frontispiece in his book, published in 1883), remembered the old windmiller of the town, a retired sea captain named Samuel Rider, who, like his mill, had very long arms. He also had an angular face, with pleasant sea-blue eyes, a large nose, and tightly compressed lips. He was not a handsome man, and he used to say facetiously that he was a warning to mothers with handsome babies, as he had been considered the handsomest one in town. In addition to his windmilling and farming, Captain Rider conducted a saltworks and a semiweekly newspaper. In politics he was a Whig, and during the Tippecanoe-and-Tyler-too campaign Mr. Rich heard him deliver an impromptu Harrison address to the fishermen engaged in packing fish at the wharf. Captain Rider, wearing heavy fisherman's boots, oilskin trousers, a green baize jacket, and sou'wester, spoke from the top of a barrel of mackerel.

"He it was," says Mr. Rich, describing the captain's activities as a miller, "who climbed the slender latticed arms and set the sail; he it was who hitched the oxen, waiting for grist, to the wheel, and with the boys pushing, turned the white wings to the wind's eye; he it was who touched the magical spring, and presto! the long wings beat the air, the great shaft began to turn, cog played to its fellow cog, and the mammoth stones began to revolve. He it was who mounted like Jove upon his Olympian seat, and one hand on the little regulator, that, better than the mills of the gods, could grind fast or slow, coarse or fine, with the other hand caught the first golden meal."

It must have been an enchanting sight to see the Cape windmills on a breezy day wrangling and gesticulating together like a congress of giants. Thoreau could hardly conceal his delight in them. He said, "The most foreign and picturesque structures on the Cape, to an inlander, not excepting the saltworks, are the windmills—gray-looking octagonal towers, with long timbers slanting to the ground in the rear, and there resting on a cart wheel, by which their fans are turned round to face the wind. These appeared also to serve in some measure for props against its force. A great circular rut was worn around the building by the wheel . . . They looked loose and slightly locomotive, like huge wounded birds, trailing a wing or leg, and reminding one of pictures of the Netherlands."

Although many of the old mills were taken down when their usefulness was gone and the material in them employed for other purposes, one reason why those which have been allowed to stand have lasted is because their frames and machinery were built of the toughest white oak, which even today rarely shows any serious cracks. Both the framework and the machinery were held together by oaken pins, scarcely any nails being used, though the village blacksmith did supply a few iron bolts and some iron straps or yokes to relieve the strain on parts of the heavy beams. The beams used in the old mill at Orleans, which was originally built at the time of the Revolution and moved to its present site in 1819, were taken from a meeting house. Notches cut for other timbers and empty dowel holes show the beams were once used in another building. It was the pegged construction of the windmills that made it relatively simple to take a mill apart and move it, though they were often moved whole. Twenty yoke of oxen were needed to haul one bodily.

A great deal of mechanical skill was required to build a windmill, and as the few millwrights available for the work could scarcely keep pace with the demand for their services, the easiest and quickest way to get a mill was to buy a secondhand one and move it. There is hardly a windmill on the Cape that has not at one time or another been moved.

The octagonal wooden towers of the ancient mills tapered upward to the cap, perhaps forty feet above the ground. Height was necessary so that the four arms, measuring as much as fifty feet from tip to tip, would clear the ground by a safe margin when under sail. The main shaft of the mill, a heavy oak timber approximately two feet thick and twenty feet long, jutted out from the dormer in the roof, and the arms passed through the exposed end of this at right angles to each other. These arms, where they joined the main shaft, usually measured ten by twelve inches. Despite the weight of the shaft and the fins, the machinery usually turned easily. In some cases it was necessary when the mill was not in operation to anchor the arms with chains hooked to staples at the corners of the mill building, as the wind turned them even when they carried no sail. This was said to be true of the old mill that stood at West Yarmouth before Henry Ford got it.

The long guide beam that extended at an angle from the rear dormer to the cart wheel on the ground was also commonly of oak. Attached to the end of this was a knee or piece of naturally curved oak forming the axle for the wheel. This axle piece and the beam were fastened together as strongly as possible with irons. The work had to be well done, as the axle and the wheel bore the weight of the beam. The wheel often ran round the mill on a circular mound of earth about one hundred feet in diameter.

The long beam and wheel are missing from the windmill at Eastham, which is the only old mill on the Cape now in working order. The top is turned by means of a cable attached to a bracket on the cap, and a truck or automobile is used to pull it around. This mill, which dates from 1793, was restored by the Works Progress Administration in 1936, and Saturday afternoons in summer, with John Fulcher playing the dusty role of miller, a couple of bags of grain are ground for the benefit of those who wish to observe one of the old wind engines in operation. It is well worth watching the sails swing around overhead in the blue windy sky and hearing the millstones going knickerbocker, knickerbocker, knickerbocker.

The caps of the mills, which were peaked, domed, or conical, did not as a rule turn on ball bearings or wheels, but in a greased groove or slot, though the cap of the Ford mill, at Dearborn, Michigan, turns on wheels over a heavily greased track. None of the Cape windmills seems to have had a guide vane or fantail, such as some English mills had, to keep the sails facing the wind.

In a maritime country like Cape Cod, which had plenty of sailmakers, the windmillers never had any difficulty getting suits of sails made for their wind-mills, and as most of them were men who had been to sea and knew what it was to handle sail up aloft in freezing weather off Cape Horn, it was nothing for them to clamber around on the skeletonic arms, setting or stowing sail. The amount of sail carried varied according to the strength of the wind, and the instinctive seamanship of the miller told him how much to use. In unfurling and furling the sails, a miller who did not know his business stood a good chance of taking a round trip and possibly getting hurt. Yet it is said to have been a stunt of Cape Cod boys to twine themselves into the latticework and loop the loop.

The interior mechanism was practically the same in all the old mills. The large wooden wheel on the main driving shaft up under the roof generally measured eight feet in diameter, and was geared to a small eighteen-inch cast-iron pinion on the vertical shaft. The millstones were driven by the gear wheel and pinion at the rate of about five and a half to one, which, while not a startling amount of power to de-velop, is not bad.

A brake in the form of a wooden friction clutch wheel around the main driving wheel was worked from the grinding room by means of ropes fixed to the ends of the brake beam. Friction applied to the rim of the large wheel gradually slowed down the sail arms until the mill stopped.

Corn was fed to the millstones by means of a wooden trough slanting down from the hopper to the hole in the middle of the upper millstone through which it dropped onto the lower stone. This trough or chute could be raised or lowered by a cord, and by slanting it more or less the flow of grain was regulated. The stones had to be fed constantly or they might rub together, generating sparks and creating a fire hazard. The old mills had a grinding capacity of about three bushels an hour, though the rate varied according to the force of the wind. The grinding room was usually on an upper floor, with the hoppers and bins to hold the grain and meal below. Corn was not the only grain milled. Barley, rye, and oats were also ground.

"I can remember," Joseph C. Lincoln said in his reminiscences of the Cape, "the groaning of the shaft as it turned and, when we went inside, the squeaking and trembling of the whole structure."

Henry C. Kittredge in his history of Cape Cod quotes a verse commemorating Thomas Baxter of Yarmouth and his sons, who were noted millwrights.

"The Baxter boys they built a mill;
  Sometimes it went, sometimes stood still;
  And when it went, it made no noise,
  Because it was built by the Baxter boys."

There is a tradition that some of the huge mill-stones were imported from Europe. Six feet in diameter and twelve or fourteen inches thick, they weighed thousands of pounds. Yet when the miller dressed the stones, the top one had to be lifted and turned. A special device for doing this was part of the equipment of most mills. It took a great deal of skill to cut the furrows or channels in the stones along which the grist worked its way out around the edges of the stones into the grinding boxes. Picking millstones is an art that is in danger of becoming lost. Householders on the Cape who succeed in getting an old millstone for a doorstep are considered fortunate.

One night some mischievous youths got hold of one of these millstones and sent it rolling down the hill at Truro. The weather was cold, the ground stiff with frost, and the great stone carried everything before it—fences, trees, and growth of all kinds. The people, hearing the rumble and crash, were alarmed, thinking the day of judgment was at hand. Fortunately, no one got in its path, nor did it strike a house, through which it would probably have gone like paper. A reward was offered for the perpetrators of the deed, but no one was caught.

Every encouragement was given to persons to build and operate windmills. Gratuities and freedom from taxation were among the inducements offered, and the miller as a rule was exempted from military and other public services. In 1697 permission was granted to set up a mill on Yarmouth common which was not to be rated, and in 1702 a gratuity of six pounds was allowed the owner for repairs. Sometimes a windmill was community owned. Barnstable in 1687 "ordered that a windmill be built, either on Cobb's Hill, or the old meeting-house hill." An appropriation of "£32 and five acres of upland and as much of marsh" was made for the purpose, and a committee of two appointed to see that the work was properly done. The windmill was built by Thomas Paine of Eastham, the greatest of the Cape millwrights. He erected others at Yarmouth, Eastham, and Truro.

Since a gristmill was in the nature of a public utility, the rate which could be charged for grinding was generally fixed by the town, the usual toll allowed being two quarts out of every bushel milled. This was known as the miller's pottle, a pottle being an old measure equal to two quarts. There were occasional complaints that a miller was overcharging. When the rate was not set by the authorities and a mill was without competition, the miller sometimes took advantage of the situation to get as much as he could. The right to establish a mill was commonly granted to a man and his heirs.

When windmills were first built on Cape Cod they were less of a curiosity than they are today. Old England had thousands of these gristmills which were perfectly familiar to the early settlers here. The English mills came in three principal styles. The earliest type known to Western Europe was the post mill, so called because the mill house with the machinery and sails was mounted on a post on which the whole body of the mill was turned to face the wind. The other two types were tower mills, one a round tower built of brick or stone, the other an octagonal wooden affair called a smock mill because of its fancied resemblance to a countryman dressed in one of the old-fashioned smocks once generally worn in rural England. Although the windmills of Cape Cod possess great individuality, all are of the smock variety, which is like the typical Dutch windmill, a design the Pilgrims were also familiar with from their years of exile in Holland.

While Cape Cod favored windmills, there were enough streams so that half the towns had watermills too, which in some places were tide mills. Tide mills were generally built at the mouths of ponds into which the tide flowed, so that the water which came in at high tide could be trapped by a dam for later release against a mill wheel. Windmills were more difficult and costly to build than watermills. Nevertheless the people of the Cape preferred them because, like schoolhouses, they could be built in any district where they were needed. Furthermore, mills on the herring rivers were apt to interfere with the spring run of alewives, a variety of fish distantly related to the herring family and the harvest of which was important to the people. In 1806 there was practically open warfare over this matter at Falmouth, where the free passage of the fish into Coonemosset Pond was prevented by a mill dam. The "herring party" went so far as to acquire a cannon, but when it burst, killing the gunner, hostilities were discontinued. Most towns, in granting mill rights, made it a condition that provision should be made, by the construction of fish runs, for the upstream migration of fish during the spawning season.

The windmills which ground grain eventually came to be outnumbered by the windmills that pumped water into the saltworks which were once numerous on the Cape. Extracting salt from sea water by solar evaporation was for several decades an important Barnstable County industry. Credit for starting the business belongs to a retired sea captain, John Sears of Dennis; when he began he was laughed at for his folly in thinking that one could get salt from the sea in commercial quantities by this method. Admittedly, the results he obtained at first were discouraging, in spite of which he went ahead with his experiments until at length he got the hang of it. Before long there were saltworks in many places on the Cape. In 1837 Provincetown had sixty-nine, Eastham fifty-four, South Yarmouth fifty-two. Hundreds of thousands of bushels of salt were made annually on the Cape.

Wars always stimulate invention, and it was the great scarcity of salt in 1776 that turned Captain Sears's attention to the problem. Salt was needed not merely for cooking and table use, but by the fishermen who used salt to cure their catches. Without salt to preserve the fish, there was little use in going fishing. Although everybody knew there was plenty of salt in the waters about Cape Cod, only Captain Sears thought of going to this obvious source for a supply.

At first the sea water was poured into the salt vats by means of buckets, but as it took three hundred and fifty gallons of water to make a bushel of salt, this was a slow and costly method. At the suggestion of another old Cape Cod salt, Captain Sears set up a windmill to pump the water at his plant, and flooding the vats was thereafter easily and quickly accomplished. With salt selling at eight dollars a bushel, the business proved highly profitable.

It took about three weeks to make a batch of salt. The windmills pumped the water through hollow logs or troughs into a range of shallow vats called water rooms. A vat generally measured thirty-six feet by eighteen, with a depth of about nine inches. It was built on piles from two to five feet above the ground, depending on the character of the soil. If loamy and wet, the vat was placed higher so as to permit the air to circulate more freely and counteract the effect of the moisture arising from the soil, which had a tendency to slow down the process. But finding a dry and sandy location on the Cape has never been a great problem. The vats were equipped with slanting movable roofs; these were removed in fair weather and replaced when it rained.

In sunny weather the sea water was kept in the first set of vats for an evaporation period of three days, by which time it had become exceedingly briny. It was then run into the second set of vats, called the pickle rooms, where crystals began to form on the surface. When this occurred, the water was drawn off into a third range of vats called salt rooms. Here the fine crystals gradually began to form into large heavy cubes which sank to the bottom. The process was now complete and the salt was raked out and stored in a dry place. The sea salt thus produced was of a good color, weighed about eighty pounds to the bushel, and was thought to be about twenty per cent stronger than the best imported salt.

After the Revolution, the price dropped from the wartime high of eight dollars a bushel, but under the embargo laws rose again to seven dollars. It was a hard blow to the Cape when its salt industry, which reached its peak in the eighteen thirties, began to decline as a result of competition from the West, of newer and less costly methods of manufacture, and of the withdrawal of the bounty. Salt continued to be made in decreasing amounts for many years, but by 1890 the business had ceased altogether.

The windmills used for the saltworks were located close to the shore, as the pumps were placed just below low-water mark. They were not so large nor so imposing as the older gristmills. The machinery was not enclosed in a tower, and the fans were mounted on a skeleton framework. In a few cases, windmills were used to grind salt. So far as I know, none of the windmills used to pump water into the saltworks has survived.

The heyday of the windmill on Cape Cod was at the beginning of the last century, when many of the older mills which later became derelict and went to wrack and ruin were still in operation and new ones were being built. In 1800 Dennis had two windmills near the meeting house and five in other parts of the town. Chatham had six. At this same time Falmouth had eight mills, one a fulling mill, the rest gristmills mostly driven by wind power. And so it went up and down the Cape. Long Island was the only place that could rival Barnstable County in the number of its windmills.

During the last quarter of the last century, summer colonists on the Cape, to whom these picturesque survivals were not just so many pieces of old machinery but a beautiful feature of the landscape, began buying windmills and moving them to their estates. They made excellent guest houses or served as quarters for members of their families, or were simply preserved as relics possessing æsthetic and antiquarian interest. One dismantled mill at the Highlands in Truro was used for many years as a lookout tower. The cap and arms were missing and a railing was built around the top. In Rich's history of Truro there is a sketch of it, with a lady on the sundeck, shielding herself with a parasol. The first windmill occupied as a dwelling seems to have been one at Wellfleet, which was converted to domestic use around the year 1870. One of the most attractive of the windmill residences is on the Herring River at West Harwich, overlooking both the river and the sea. Its situation near the water makes it look like a windmill on an old Dutch china clock.

More than half a century ago J. J. E. Rothery bought two old windmills which he moved to his summer place at Cataumet on Buzzards Bay. One of these mills came from the vicinity of New Bedford, where it was originally built in 1745. His daughter, Agnes Rothery, the author of many books, wrote a novel, *The House by the Windmill*, in which this mill, with its quaint Dutch roof tucked in under the eaves, is described. Outwardly it is perfect, but within it is devoid of machinery. When first moved to Cataumet, its interior was festooned with cobwebs swinging from the huge beams, while its floors were splintered and broken by the falling millstones. "The queer winding steps, narrow and crude, which led from the first floor to the second, and the second to the third, were almost worn through by the pressure of feet long since departed. The oak handrail was polished as smooth as ivory by the touch of fingers long since folded in quietness."

In the absence of a Society for the Preservation of Ancient Windmills, this latter-day use of the old towers undoubtedly has been the means of saving a number from neglect and ruin.

In 1935, the price of secondhand windmills rose sharply when it was learned that the Ford dealers of America had purchased the oldest one on the Cape and planned to move it to Michigan as a present to Henry Ford and Edsel B. Ford. There was a storm of protest, but all pleas to let Cape Cod keep its ancient mill were unavailing. While the action of the owner was severely criticized, it was partly the fault of the town of Yarmouth that the mill was lost to the Cape. Although the old relic had been repeatedly offered to the town, the selectmen took no action, even though they were aware of its value as a historical asset. Despite the fact that it was something in the nature of a public monument, they would neither exempt it from taxation, nor assist in its upkeep. Vexed by their attitude, the owner finally decided to sell it, and America's oldest windmill was moved to Dearborn, where it is now one of the exhibits in the Ford show place at Greenfield Village.

This was not the first time the aged mill had migrated. Built by the Plymouth Pilgrims in 1633, it was moved in 1750 to Bass River Village on the Cape, thence in 1782 to South Yarmouth, and in 1894 to West Yarmouth, where it was known as the Farris mill. It was not taken apart for the journey from South Yarmouth to West Yarmouth, but was moved bodily. To Michigan, however, it was transported in pieces, even to the stonework of the base. Since the mill was a gift to the Fords, there is no record at Dearborn of the purchase price or the cost of moving and restoration.

The one-hundred-and-fifty-year-old windmill on the hill at Chatham is believed to have inspired and been the model for the first toy windmill made on Cape Cod. Countless thousands of these brightly-painted wooden weathervanes have been sold as souvenirs to summer visitors during the past forty years. Arthur Wilson Tarbell says in his book, *Cape Cod Ahoy!,* that Captain Herbert Eldredge of the Chatham Life Saving Station originated the idea when he made one for a young relative in Chatham. A summer visitor happened to see it and requested him to make windmills for his sons. Similar requests were made by others and soon the men at the station were kept busy during their spare time filling orders, until the government heard of it and put a stop to the business. Joseph C. Lincoln's novel, *Shavings,* in which he tells the story of a Yankee whittler who made these models in his home workshop, did much to make these small mills known, and the manufacture of them became one of the Cape's minor industries.

It was the high-speed, steam-powered gristmills equipped with steel rollers, as well as the improvement of transportation facilities, that finally put a quietus on the old Cape Cod custom of building windmills. Today, one no longer sees them beckoning across the dunes with half-human gestures, nor hears the cheerful clatter of their sails, or the millstones going knickerbocker, knickerbocker, knickerbocker.

CAPE COD has always had good "housen." Long ago it established a tradition of seacoast building that has become definitely associated with its name. The so-called Cape Cod house is a distinctive and easily recognizable type known to everyone. It is unaffected in feeling, has strength of line and economy of design, and has about it that difference which distinguishes it from the ordinary run of landsmen's houses.

Exigencies of the site dictated the form these houses took. Situated on a peninsula that was apt to be windswept and storm-beaten, they were constructed with maritime efficiency to withstand the most outrageous weather conditions. Built broad and low, they hugged the sandy earth closely. Usually, the houses were placed in valleys or hollows formed by the sand hills, like buttons on overstuffed upholstery, which gave them a certain measure of natural protection from the elements, and they were generally located near some inlet or harbor, since the sea provided the inhabitants with a large part of their sustenance.

The houses belonging to this tradition were described by Timothy Dwight, who visited the Cape a century and a half ago. He said, "These have one story, and four rooms on the lower floor; and are covered on the sides, as well as the roof, with pine shingles, eighteen inches in length. The chimney is in the middle, immediately behind the front door; and on each side of the door are two windows. The roof is straight. Under it are two chambers; and there are two larger, and two smaller, windows in the gable end. This is the general structure, and appearance, of the great body of houses from Yarmouth to Race Point. There are, however, several varieties, but of too little importance to be described. A great proportion of them are in good repair. Generally, they exhibit a tidy, neat aspect in themselves, and in their appendages; and furnish proof of comfortable living, by which I was at once disappointed and gratified. The barns are usually neat, but always small."

The typical Cape Cod house as a rule was shingled rather than clapboarded, because shingles were supposed to keep a place warmer, and more often than not they were left unpainted. Exposure to the sun and the salt air soon turned them to a soft, silvery gray, with a touch of moss occasionally giving a bluish-green tinge. Sometimes the roof was painted red, while the walls were left to color naturally. If the whole house was given a coat, the front might be white and the ends red, or some other combination of colors. White lead was expensive in colonial times, as it was imported from abroad, and perhaps all a family could afford was enough to paint the front, which was often clapboarded. Blue was also popular on the Cape, a not unsatisfactory stain being made by mixing blue clay with skimmed milk; but natural paintless gray is the traditional Cape color.

It used to be said that while Cape Cod folk were not cold-blooded, they were careful, and in the days of sail a girl would not dance with the mate if she could dance with the captain. This was perhaps taking a sound and sensible view of the matter, because in a cold and somewhat bleak country like the Cape, the captain's house was apt to have amenities the mate's had not, and women could scarcely fail to note that they had to live mostly indoors. But since

promotion went by merit, the odds favored the captain as being the better man, and as such entitled to
the prettiest girl.

Most newly married couples, however, started
modestly enough by building only half a house, with
two front windows and the door at one side of these
and the chimney behind the door. As the family increased in size, they built on to the house on the side
next to the door, making a three-quarter house by
adding one window, or a whole house if the addition
included two windows. The door in the course of this
development moved from one side to a central position between the four front windows. Sometimes
there were more windows than this across the front,
but the usual number was four. If after the full house
was completed more room still was needed, ells were
added if the owner could afford extensions. Exam-
ples of the half, the three-quarter, and the full house
are to be seen on the Cape today.

The roofs and floors of dismantled saltworks were
used to build barns, outbuildings, and even houses.
Freeman in his *History of Cape Cod* (1860) says that
strangers visiting places where the salt industry had
declined noticed a peculiarity in the appearance of
barns and other outbuildings, which was described
by a visitor as "a sort of fancy-stained, rust-spotted,
regularly-patterned boarding, which, from its fre-
quency, comes to haunt the observer and demand
explanation." Freeman says that these boards were

from the old saltworks and the rust was that of nails spread by the action of the salt. These nails were driven in a peculiar pattern when the saltworks were built, hence the odd appearance of the buildings in which this boarding was afterward incorporated.

A good deal of serviceable building material used to be washed up by the sea and ship timbers and other parts of wrecks were used in the construction of many Cape Cod houses. Thoreau noted that beside almost every house he saw there was laid up a spar or plank or two full of augur holes, saved from some wreck. The lighthouse keeper with whom he stayed told him that he made three thousand singles from a mast for use in shingling his barn. The spindle on the steeple of the Chatham Congregational Church, says Jack Johnson in *Cape Cod Stories*, was made from a spar from the bark *R. A. Allen*, which was wrecked on the Chatham sand bars in 1887, during the same storm in which the church spire was damaged by lightning. In heavy weather, Maine lumber schooners sometimes lost part of their deckloads of laths, shingles, or boards, and high water along the rivers of Maine often washed great quantities of logs and lumber down to the sea, much of which the long arm of the Cape gathered in for the benefit of the inhabitants. Building material was expensive and nothing was ever wasted.

Once a furnished house was cast up on the sands of the Cape. It had been washed from its foundations on Haley's Island, one of the Isles of Shoals, off Portsmouth, New Hampshire. A box containing papers and other articles supplied the clue to its identity. The family, it is said, had just had time to escape, but as it turned out they could have remained and journeyed safely to the Cape. Perhaps because it was small and not what is sometimes called an ark of a house, this seagoing dwelling withstood the voyage very well. The spot where it stood on Haley's Island used to be pointed out to visitors.

Deacon John Dyer of Provincetown was a great mover of buildings. When the settlement at Long Point, the long, sandy spit protecting Provincetown Harbor, was abandoned, the deacon moved, on scows, most of the houses across the harbor to the town. Today there is nothing on the Point except the lighthouse, which marks the extreme tip of Cape Cod and the entrance to Provincetown, but at one time thirty-eight families lived there. Not only was it handy to the fishing grounds, but there were plenty of fish to be caught from the shore, and it was a good location for the extensive saltworks located there. The first house was built in 1818. After the lighthouse was erected in 1827, school was kept in it. A regular schoolhouse, which was also used as a church, was built and opened in 1848, with sixty scholars in attendance. But the village occupied an exposed situation and the water supply was poor. In dry weather drinking water had to be brought across the harbor in casks. The movement back to town began about 1850, and by the outbreak of the Civil War only two houses besides the schoolhouse were left. Finally, the school was floated across from the Point. Converted to other uses, it still stands on Commercial Street in Provincetown.

A curiosity of Cape building was the cellars. As in other parts of New England, these did not as a rule extend under the whole house, but only part way; and here, as elsewhere, they were often lined with stone, which in some cases came as ballast in vessels. Many of the old houses on the Lower Cape, however, have round cellars built of brick imported from the mainland. The circular form was used to prevent the pressure of the shifting sand from forcing in the walls. These round, cisternlike cellars, according to Thoreau, were only nine to twelve feet in diameter, and were cheap to build, as a single thickness of brick was sufficient even for cellars of larger dimensions. But there was not much necessity for large cellars on the Lower Cape, because few vegetables were raised to put in them. At Provincetown, in the days when they built their houses on stilts to let the sand blow under them, no attempt was made to have cellars.

Wells were also built round for the same reason, with the bucket customarily raised and lowered in nautical style with a block and tackle, though once in a while an old spar was used as a sweep.

One gets the impression from many of the old story-and-a-half Cape houses that it would be impossible to move around in the upper story without knocking one's head against the beams or to look out the windows without crawling around on all fours. But this lowness does not seem to have bothered the Cape Codders, perhaps because they were a seagoing folk accustomed to the limited headroom of ships' forecastles and cabins. The stairway leading to the attic in the old houses is frequently as steep and narrow as a companionway, which one ascends or descends with one hand touching a rope. The children usually slept in the half-story.

Thoreau was amused by the number of windows in the gable ends of the Cape cottages. Looking for a lodging for the night at Wellfleet, he came across several sober-looking houses which, to judge from the array of windows, he concluded had room for him. "The great number of windows in the ends of the houses," he wrote, "and their irregularity in size and position, here and elsewhere on the Cape, struck us agreeably,—as if each of the various occupants who had their *cunabula* behind had punched a hole where his necessities required it, and, according to his size and stature, without regard to the outside effect. There were windows for the grown folks, and windows for the children,—three or four apiece; as a certain man had a large hole cut in his barn-door for the cat, and another smaller one for the kitten.

Sometimes they were so low under the eaves that I thought they must have perforated the plate beam for another apartment, and I noticed some which were triangular, to fit that part more exactly. The ends of the houses had thus as many muzzles as a revolver, and, if the inhabitants have the same habit of staring out the windows that some of our neighbors have, a traveller must stand a small chance with them."

The roofs of the houses present a marked characteristic of Cape architecture. On the old houses they come down so low that some people have gained the impression that Cape Codders must have been a race of little people, which, of course, is the opposite of the truth. With the first story usually not more than seven feet high, the roof exhibits a rather large expanse of shingles, and this is perhaps even more marked on the northerly side of the salt-box houses, with their long lean-to roofs descending to a line barely six feet above the ground. The roomier gambrel roof is not common to the Cape, nor is the arched rainbow roof often seen.

This last, sometimes called the ship's-bottom, whaleback, or hog's-back roof, rises from the eaves to the ridge pole in a curve resembling the bottom of a boat, or, if you like, the arc of a rainbow. The most famous example on the Cape is the Rainbow House at West Falmouth, which is thought to be over two hundred and fifty years old. It belonged originally to Thomas Bowerman, a Quaker, who because of his beliefs got into trouble with the authorities and was jailed. There is a tradition that the first child born in Falmouth came into being on a bed of bulrushes beneath an overturned boat and because of the unusual circumstances of his birth was named Moses—Moses Hatch. This was perhaps the first rainbow roof to give shelter on the Cape.

The front door was naturally the focal point of the house and the one place where adornment was permissible. Everything else was usually kept severely plain until it came to the door; there all the decoration was centered. Here the local builder let himself go, with singularly delightful results. The door more often than not was made with six panels symbolically arranged to form a cross and for this reason called by some people a Christian door. With a fan light or side lights or both, and with beautifully designed pilasters supporting, perhaps, a Greek pediment, the Cape doorway is charming in both detail and general effect. The Greek influence is visibly strong everywhere on the Cape.

Door latches were frequently used with the cusps in a swordfish design. The weathervanes to be seen on barns or outbuildings also commonly took the form of some species of fish or whale.

Inside, the wide-cut pine floor boards were scoured as white as snow and then sanded with salt-white sand which was swept into a herringbone pattern.

In some houses the sand was left in islands, as on a map, to teach the boys how to steer an intricate course. In well-disciplined families these sandy archipelagos remained intact for days.

Plaster now comes like cake mix and with the addition of sand and water is easily made, but the early Cape Codders, lacking anything of the kind, ground up clam and oyster shells, which are full of lime, to make their noted clam-shell plaster. Accumulations of shells at places where the Indians had for generations gone to feast on shellfish proved a boon to the first builders; they burned the shells for lime to make mortar with which to build the huge central chimneys that are a feature of the typical Cape Cod house. Town records show that the taking of shells from the Indian dumps was strictly regulated.

One of the peculiarities of Cape Cod residences noticed by travelers as presenting a contrast to other parts of the country was that well-to-do people lived in small, unpretentious houses which in no way indicated that they were any better off than their neighbors.

"Few dwellings on Cape Cod cost over $1,000," remarked one commentator of the earlier part of the last century, "yet there are many wealthy men who live in houses of this cost—men, too, whose families are highly educated, and whose sons and daughters visit and marry in the best circles of society of Boston and New York."

While this democratic simplicity and equality in the style of their buildings was probably largely true, there were many exceptions, as any one may see by surviving houses that obviously represent a far greater outlay, though none of them is ostentatious. What the writer intended to say was that Cape Cod had no codfish aristocracy. Newly rich people in New England were often called codfish aristocracy when their wealth made them act as if they were superior to ordinary folk who had been less successful. Quick fortunes were sometimes made in the fishing industry, particularly on the Cape, where a family in humble circumstances might wake to find that the head of the household had returned from a trip with a fare of codfish worth many thousands of dollars. One of the most remarkable catches was that of William McKay of Provincetown, who in 1882 returned from three months' fishing on the Grand Banks with 4,400 quintals of cod worth twenty-two thousand dollars. A whale ship might return after a much longer absence with a cargo of oil and ambergris several times more valuable. Plenty of envy and the attitude that money isn't everything were behind the phrase which took the lowly cod instead of some lordly fish for a symbol. But the days when the appellation could be used accurately have gone, and it is now generally used of persons who feel superior to their position.

"Generally," said Thoreau, "the old-fashioned

and unpainted houses on the Cape looked more comfortable, as well as picturesque, than the modern and more pretending ones, which were less in harmony with the scenery, and less firmly planted."

The larger houses on the Cape belonging to prosperous searfaring families often had a captain's walk on the roof commanding a view of the water. Old houses with this distinctly maritime architectural feature still exist on Cape Cod. In 1807, Kendall, the visiting Englishman, saw a woman at Provincetown with her son on top of a sand dune, looking through a telescope for the fishing vessel of her husband, the sand hill serving her for a lookout quite as well as a rooftop promenade. It is very easy to visualize her standing there, with the small boy beside her, her skirt whipping about her in the wind as she scans the horizon with her glass. At Eastham, Kendall stopped at a house which had a roof walk, and went up for a look around.

"As I traveled the road through Eastham on my journey downward," he says, "I left on my right a glittering mansion, white and black, that rose above the level of the champaign by which it was surrounded, and appeared to be the chateau of the domain. On making inquiries concerning it, I learned it belonged to Captain Collings, and that I might well be entertained in it on my return."

On his way back he stopped there to dine, and after dinner his host showed him over his lands. "Then,"

Kendall continues, "I was led upstairs to view the apartments of the house, the new painting, and the wainscoats; and lastly ascended to the gallery on the roof, carrying with us a telescope. In our way, the captain called my particular attention to a small bed-chamber, which he described as an exceedingly desirable lodging room. On the roof he made me observe all the flat and naked land adjacent, with its hollows and tracts of marsh; and then the blue ocean by which, to the southward, the whole is bounded: 'Now, sir,' said he, 'if you know any gentleman of fortune, that has traveled a great deal, and wishes to enjoy retirement, I should be very glad if you would recommend this spot to him; you see what a comfortable bed-chamber there is below; and we have plenty of fishing, and plenty of snipe and plover.' "

Kendall made an amusing discovery when he visited the Indian town of Mashpee. Naturally the Indians originally followed the old tribal custom of living in wigwams, but eventually built houses after the fashion of those they saw about them. Kendall found the greater part of the Mashpee Indians living in wooden houses. One family, however, had a wigwam, and this, oddly enough, did not belong to an Indian but to an Englishman named Macregor, a native of Manchester, England, who was one of the wealthier residents of the village. He had become a squaw man and apparently lived quite happily with his dumpy Indian wife in a tepee.

"This man," Kendall remarks, "is in possession of a very respectable farm and orchard, both of which are particularly well attended. His land is close to the sea, and he is employed in ditching and embanking a tract of marsh, which is at present too much exposed to the tide, and though he lives in no solitude, and is not without the assistance of as many hands as he finds it convenient to employ, yet his enterprise, his situation, his wigwam, and the complete state of order observable around it, his straw hat, and general personal appearance, made me regard him as a second Robinson Crusoe. He informed me that he left Manchester before he was ten years of age, and followed a sailor's life till he was twenty. At that time, which is now twenty-seven years ago, he married his present wife. He has lived on the plantation ever since, but has no children. From others, I heard, that when he first came to the neighborhood, he had a stock of clothes, though in other respects destitute; and that his situation was not so bad, but that he might have married into a respectable family, almost as easy as into an Indian. I thought it a little singular, that while almost everyone of the Indians had a wooden house, this Englishman was lodged in a wigwam; but the wigwam agrees with the taste of his wife, and his own attention seems to be given exclusively to his farm and garden."

The Indian Mission Church at Mashpee, built in 1684, is the Cape's oldest church. A plain, white, clapboarded structure set among the pines, it looks more like a schoolhouse than a church, but inside are the old box pews and an organ loft. It was remodeled in 1717, and comparing the building as it appears today with the picture of it in Barber's *Massachusetts Historical Collections*, published in 1839, it is apparent that the exterior has been altered since Barber's time.

Cape Cod did its best to follow the old New England custom of building its meeting houses on the most elevated sites it could find. Towns were proud of their churches and liked to put them where everybody could see them. Along what John Masefield calls "the strange curving crook of Cape Cod," the meeting houses served as landmarks for vessels on the bay and ships at sea. The last glimpse many a Cape Cod mariner had of his native town was the church on the hill.

The Truro meeting house was perhaps the most famous of all the Cape landmarks in the early days. The heavy white-oak frame of this church, which was replaced in 1840 after one hundred and nineteen years of service, was cut on the site and when the timbers were removed they were as sound as ever. In connection with this meeting house, it is pleasant to recall the elderly deacon whose duty it was to supply the communion bread and wine. The first Sunday of every month he rode his old white horse up the sandy road to the meeting house with the sacramental jug hanging from his saddle. It is less pleasant to recall the ironical death of Amos Sellew of Boston, a native of Truro, who was liquidated near Pond Landing, October 16, 1856, aged forty-one. While engaged in unloading from the packet in which he was a passenger an iron fence for his burial lot in the yard of the Truro meeting house, the vessel suddenly sank, taking Mr. Sellew and his ironmongery to the bottom.

The steeple of the old parish meeting house at Yarmouth was another important landmark, particularly for vessels going into Yarmouth or Barnstable harbors on the bay side.

In 1712 the town of Sandwich voted that the selectmen should get the glass for the meeting house mended, the shutters hung to the windows, the latches of the doors mended, a lock procured, and they were also to reason with John Tracy about his work and charges for setting up the turret on the meeting house.

The collector of antique meeting houses and old churches can add some fine specimens to his collection in Barnstable County. But after all it is the

houses which give Cape Cod its special atmosphere.
They are the real museum pieces. The Cape tradition
of building produced a house that was admirably
suited to its surroundings. It was straightforward
and without nuance, but never lacking in romance.

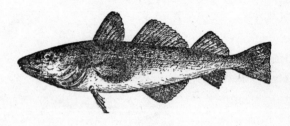

IT USED to be a New England point of honor to eat salt codfish. Palfrey says the most ceremonious Boston feast was never set out on Saturday, which was the common dinner-party day, without dun fish at one end of the table. Men pleased themselves while eating it with the thought that they were doing their part to maintain the fisheries and create a naval strength.

Saturday, not Friday, was observed as fish day

throughout New England up to the time of the Civil War. The custom was a survival from the days of Queen Elizabeth, who to encourage her seamen had a law passed in 1563 which ordered the eating of fish on Wednesdays and Saturdays. So well-established was the custom of the piscatorial Saturday that a Massachusetts court took judicial notice of it.

Salt codfish were what Thoreau saw stacked up on the wharves of Provincetown, "looking like corded wood, maple and yellow birch with the bark left on." He did not himself taste fresh fish, he said, while on the Cape. Codfish were then generally salted, the smallest being cured for the foreign market, the largest for home consumption. They were exposed on the flakes until thoroughly dried and turned a reddish brown. They were called dun fish and were highly esteemed as food. An appetizing dish with the unappetizing name of "hog's-back son of a sea cook" was made of salted codfish cooked with pork scraps.

According to Thoreau, the houses of Provincetown were closely beset by the wooden flakes on which the fish were spread to dry, "leaving only a narrow passage two or three feet wide to the front door; so that instead of looking out into a flower or grass plot, you looked on to so many square rods of cod turned wrong side outwards." These parterres, he adds, smelled least like a flower garden on a good drying day in summer. There were flake yards all over the Cape in those days, and in the cod-fishing season acres of cod were exposed on them for curing in the sun. At other times it was other fish.

Fresh cod was eaten, of course, on the vessels whose crews caught the fish. The fishermen were particularly partial to the tongues and sounds. The tongue is not literally the tongue of the fish, but a piece of flesh taken from the base of it, and the sounds are cut from the jowls. Until well along into the nineteenth century the cooking arrangements on fishing vessels were extremely crude. Vessels were equipped with a small brick fireplace and plastered wooden chimney in the cabin or cuddy. The chimney came out flush with the deck, and when a fire was built below a square wooden funnel was added above. The Gloucester hood for chimneys was then unheard of, and no one could safely predict which way the smoke would go, whether up or down. But the tendency of the chimneys to smoke gave the fishermen, particularly in the Grand Bankers, some of the most delicious smoked halibut imaginable. When a particularly fine specimen was caught, the choicest cuts were taken and hung from the beams in the cabin, where by the end of the voyage they had been smoked to a turn. The halibut thus cured was divided among the crew, who took it home or gave it to appreciative friends.

Lighting the fire in the cuddy was a disagreeable job when homemade matches dipped in brimstone had to be ignited by the flint-and-steel method. In rough weather the smell of the brimstone was enough to make a person who felt the least bit squeamish actively ill. If the vessel were really rolling, it was impossible to cook anything. After stoves came in, a huge wave once threw the stove on a fishing schooner into the berth with the cook.

Portuguese and Negroes were favored as cooks. The cook usually made more money than the ordinary hands on a fishing vessel. A writer on the New England fisheries said many years ago of the Portuguese, "They make good stewards, being industrious and very fond of the perquisites which fall to the lot of those who hold this position, receiving not only a full share with the men, but additional compensation for their services, and other privileges which they are not slow to take advantage of."

The bill of fare on the fishing vessels naturally consisted mostly of fish. The stores taken on board for a crew of three men going on an offshore fishing trip lasting from two days to a week were two quarts of molasses, five pounds of fat pork, four pounds of flour, seven pounds of hard bread, half a barrel of water, and a supply of New England rum, which was considered as much a part of the victuals as anything. The Porto Rican molasses used was called Porty Reek long lick. No elaborate meals could be gotten up by the cook from such limited supplies, but the men seem to have been satisfied.

Among the odd concoctions which the fisherman

liked to eat was Dundee pudding, made by pounding up hard bread, sweetening it with molasses, and stirring a little flour into the mixture. It was, of course, not like real Dundee pudding. Another standby dish was hard bread, or pilot biscuit, fried in pork fat.

A holiday mess for fishermen was fummadiddle, which, as one might guess from the name, was a compound mixture. It was a kind of mush, composed of stale bread, pork fat and scraps, molasses, water, with cinnamon, allspice, and cloves by way of seasoning, baked in the oven, and placed on the table hot and brown. The baking was done in a Dutch oven which hung from a crossbar in the chimney. Coals were heaped on the flat top of the oven and, aided by the coals in the fireplace underneath, dishes were baked on both sides.

As a special treat, the cook made pancakes with beach plums in them called joe floggers. A modern version of this old seagoing favorite can be made as follows:

JOE FLOGGERS

Use your favorite pancake batter or mix. Add sliced beach plums, and fry in the usual way on a heavy griddle or frying pan. If you lack the beach plums, substitute sliced peeled apples. Although they didn't have it on fishing vessels, be sure to serve joe floggers with maple syrup.

The Portuguese on the Cape have always liked pickled fish, and a popular formula for doing this is called *vinha d'alhos,* which takes its name from the two principal ingredients used, namely, vinegar and garlic.

VINHA D'ALHOS

Combine three-quarters cup of vinegar with two and a half cups of water, two minced sections of garlic, one-half teaspoon cumin seed, three-quarters teaspoon salt, and one-half teaspoon black pepper. Cut the fish into pieces suitable for serving. Let stand twelve hours in the refrigerator. Drain and dry on absorbent paper. Roll in corn meal and fry.

This process should not be used with mackerel, herring, or other strong, fatty fish, but it is suited to the various flounders.

There has come down to us from the olden times an account of what the inhabitants of Cape Cod used to eat in their homes, and from it one would say that they were a very comfortably victualled people. The report, which is from a description of the town of Chatham published in 1802, is brief enough to be quoted.

"Food can so easily be procured, either on the shore or in the sea, that, with the profit which arises from their voyages, in which it must be confessed they labor very hard, the people are enabled to cover their tables well with provisions. A breakfast among the inhabitants, and even among those who are called the poorest, for there are none which may be called really poor, consists of tea or coffee, brown bread, generally with butter, sometimes without, salt or fresh fish, fried or broiled. A dinner affords one or more of the following dishes: fresh roots and herbs; salted beef or pork boiled; fresh butcher's meat not more than twelve times a year; wild fowl frequently in the autumn and winter; fresh fish boiled or fried with pork; shell fish; salt fish boiled; Indian pudding; pork baked with beans. Tea or coffee also frequently constitutes part of the dinner. A supper consists of tea or coffee, and fish, as at breakfast; cheese, cakes made of flour, gingerbread, and pies of several sorts. This bill of fare will serve, with little variation, for all the fishing towns in the county. In many families there is no difference between breakfast and supper; cheese, cakes, and pies being common at the one as at the other."

Eating fish is such an ancient Cape Cod custom that it is not surprising that the art of preparing it has been carried to perfection there, not only in the case of the fishes of the sea, but also those of the shore. Superb sea food in agreeable variety is, indeed, one of the goodly heritages of the Cape, and the traditional ways of preparing it are infinite. Justifiably, entire books have been devoted to Cape cookery. An excellent one for sea food is a paper-bound booklet published in Provincetown called *Vittles for the Captain* by Harriet Adams, with informing and amusing comments on the recipes by N. M. Halper.

Gourmets quite properly insist that the best way

to serve a sizable fish is to bake or roast it whole. Prepared in this way every bit of the delicate juicy flavor of the tender flesh is brought out. One of the masterpieces of the region's cuisine is Cape Cod "Turkey," which is a stuffed cod or haddock baked whole and brought to the table in full majesty. This truly imperial dish is prepared in the following manner:

CAPE COD "TURKEY" WITH SAVORY STUFFING

Select a four-pound fish, with the head and tail left on, cleaned and prepared for baking. Wipe the fish with a damp cloth and rub with seasoning mixture inside and out. Stuff with savory stuffing and sew together or fasten with skewers. Put a few gashes on top of fish and place strips of salt pork or bacon in the gashes.

Preheat the oven to 400°F. and oil the baking pan well. Place an oiled cheesecloth in the pan and lay the fish on it. Brush fish with salad oil or butter and bake nine minutes per pound if the head is left on, twelve minutes per pound if the head is off.

When the fish is done, remove to the platter by lifting the fish in the cheesecloth. Garnish with parsley and serve with wedges of lime or lemon. A four-pound cod or haddock will serve four to six persons.

Savory stuffing: Mix together one cup bread crumbs, one-half cup melted butter or margarine, one-half cup hot water, one-quarter teaspoon salt, one-half teaspoon of sage, one-half onion minced, one-eighth teaspoon pepper.

As for shellfish, here is a method of preparing clams which is thought by many to be one of the best ways of eating them. Certainly they are very good when prepared according to this recipe.

CLAM CAKES

Combine one pint loose clams put through the chopper with two beaten eggs, two and a half tablespoons flour, one-fourth teaspoon salt, and one-fourth teaspoon pepper. Shape into flat cakes, each containing one tablespoonful of the mixture. Dip in flour and fry in butter until brown. Then turn to brown the other side.

Chowder, which is called the monarch of the stews, is said to have originated in France and reached New England through the Breton fishermen of Newfoundland, who were in the habit of cooking fish mixed with other ingredients in a caldron (*chaudière*), as they had done at home in France. Wherever it came from, chowder has been a Cape Cod institution since time immemorial. Clam chowder can be made in a variety of ways, but on the Cape they follow the orthodox New England practice of not using tomatoes. After all, Yankees had consumed chowder by the kettleful for a couple of centuries before anyone dreamed of eating a tomato, and they could not bring themselves to ruin a good chowder with this upstart fruit. One expert I know claims that the secret of making good chowder, whether clam or fish chowder, is to use condensed milk; I have eaten a haddock chowder made in this way it would be difficult to beat.

Cape Cod oysters are justly famous, particularly the Wellfleet and Cotuit oysters. In the days when there were oyster stands and oyster houses throughout New England, most of them were operated by Wellfleet men who were supplied with oysters from their native town.

When Thoreau stayed with Uncle Jack Newcomb, the ancient Wellfleet oysterman, he had eels for breakfast. At his hotel in Provincetown the landlord asked him if he would take hashed fish or beans. He took the beans, though he said they were never a favorite dish of his. The next summer this was still the only alternative for breakfast at the hotel. In the hash he found a remarkable proportion of fish. "As you travel inland," he remarked, "the potato predominates." Presumably, at the hotel a stove was used to bake the beans and fry the fish hash, but breakfast at the oysterman's in Wellfleet was prepared primitively in the fireplace, and Thoreau's account of it is one of the more diverting passages in his Cape Cod book.

"Before sunrise the next morning," he says, "they let us out again, and I ran over to the beach to see the sun come out of the ocean. The old woman of eighty-four winters was already out in the cold morning wind, bareheaded, tripping about like a young girl, and driving up the cow to milk. She got the breakfast with despatch, and without noise or bustle; and meanwhile the old man resumed his stories, standing before us, who were sitting, with his back to the chimney, and ejecting his tobacco-juice right and left into the fire behind him, without regard to the various dishes which were there preparing. At breakfast we had eels, buttermilk cake, cold bread, green beans, doughnuts, and tea. The old man talked a steady stream; and when his wife told him he had better eat his breakfast, he said: 'Don't hurry me; I have lived too long to be hurried.' I ate of the apple-sauce and the doughnuts, which I thought had sustained the least detriment from the old man's shots, but my companion refused the apple-sauce, and ate of the hot cake and green beans, which had appeared to him to occupy the safest part of the hearth. But on comparing notes afterward, I told him that the buttermilk cake was particularly exposed, and I saw how it suffered repeatedly, and therefore I avoided it; but he declared that, however that might be, he witnessed that the apple-sauce was seriously injured, and had therefore declined that."

The local fresh water eels of the Cape are considered to be a great delicacy. How they were prepared by the oysterman's wife, I do not know, but here is the way to cook them in Cape Cod style.

FRIED EELS

Skin and clean the eels. Cut in two-inch pieces. Cover with boiling water, and boil eight minutes. Sprinkle with salt and pepper. Dip in corn meal, and sauté in pork or bacon fat.

The applesauce which formed part of the Wellfleet breakfast was undoubtedly made of apples grown by the old oysterman himself. "He gave us to taste what he called the Summer Sweeting," says Thoreau, "a pleasant apple which he raised, and frequently grafted from, but had never seen growing elsewhere, except once,—three trees on Newfoundland, or at the Bay of Chaleur, I forget which, as he was sailing by. He was sure he could tell the tree at a distance."

There are still growing in Wellfleet apple trees which were washed ashore as nursery stock from the wreck of the *Franklin,* shortly before Thoreau's visit a century ago. And Timothy Dwight, who rode his horse along the sandy roads of the Cape in the year 1800, says there were several good apple orchards in Sandwich, where the only cider mill on Cape Cod was then located.

One summer morning in 1807 Edward Kendall stopped for breakfast at Barnstable and found all the men in town had gone to the salt marshes to make hay. At the public house where he paused for refreshment, the women told him they were at their second breakfast, having eaten their first at three o'clock in the morning, when they fed the men before they went to work.

Alewives which hung from the rafters of Cape Cod barns were common at breakfast, as was a dried salted cousin of this fish called slit herring. Fortune stew was a dish of small, round potatoes served whole in a milk gravy. Fish and potatoes were the highliners of the Cape Cod menu.

It would be gross negligence not to mention the fruit of Cape Cod, especially the cranberries. But first a word about the blueberries. They are as good here as anywhere in New England. They do especially well on land where the pitch-pine woods have been burned. In Maine they deliberately burn the blueberry barrens, but on the Cape the pitch-pine forest fires are always accidental. Yet there are some who believe that, regardless of the ordeal by fire, the world's best-flavored blueberries are to be found on the Cape.

"The Narrow Land," declares the *Boston Herald*, paying tribute to the Cape Cod blueberry, "is blessed with gentle climate and soft winds; its thin soil is just what blueberries need for best development. The deep purple bloom on the clusters of dark jewels is compounded of sun-blessed days and starlit nights. Furthermore, Cape Codders know how to make a pie. They pour the foundation of lower crust thick enough so one can remove a wedge without disaster. They put sugar and flour on the bottom crust so one has a crunchy, crystallized goodness to blend with the filling. They scatter some flour over the berries so the juice will be thick and they toss on a scattering of butter dots before the top crust is tucked tight. Hot or cold, from breakfast to bedtime, blueberry pie made Cape Cod style is a valid reason for calling this the good old summer time."

The more famous Cape Cod cranberry needs no bush. It is a versatile berry which can in one way or another be used appropriately at any time from the beginning to the end of a meal. It can be used as an appetizer, as a sauce, jelly, or relish, and for desserts. Cranberries can be easily and quickly prepared. There is no peeling or coring. Everything about the berry, including its looks and its flavor, is good. But cranberries should never be cooked in anything but earthen, porcelain-lined, or enameled vessels, and after cooking should be placed in glass or earthenware dishes only.

There are several ways of making cranberry sauce, which is almost as good with beef, lamb, pork, or veal as it is with turkey. Its touch of tartness makes it particularly acceptable when served with fatty meats. Cranberry sauce may be made straight, stewed, or strained.

CRANBERRY SAUCE

One quart cranberries, two cups sugar, two cups water. Boil the sugar and water together five minutes. Add cranberries and boil without stirring until all the skins pop open. Five minutes over a hot fire is usually sufficient. Remove from fire when the popping stops and leave the sauce in the saucepan until cool. This makes one quart of sauce.

STEWED CRANBERRY SAUCE

One quart cranberries, two cups water, two cups sugar. Cook the cranberries and water about twenty minutes or until all the skins are broken. Then add the sugar and simmer for five minutes more. Chill thoroughly before serving.

STRAINED CRANBERRY SAUCE

Four cups cranberries, two cups water, one to one and one-half cups sugar. Boil the berries and water until all the skins are broken. Press through a coarse strainer, keeping back the skins. Add the sugar and cook until sugar is dissolved.

CRANBERRY JELLY

Eight quarts (eight pounds) cranberries and two and one-half pounds sugar will make ten glasses of jelly. Cook the cranberries until soft, using three cups of water for each eight cups of berries. Strain the juice through a jelly bag. Measure the juice, heat to boiling point, and add one cup of sugar for each two cups of juice. Stir until the sugar is dissolved; boil briskly for five minutes. Pour into glass tumblers, porcelain or crockery molds, and cover with paraffin.

CRANBERRY MUFFINS

One cup cranberries, one-half cup sugar, two cups flour, four teaspoons baking powder, three-quarters teaspoon salt, one egg beaten, one cup milk, three tablespoons melted butter.

Put the cranberries through the food chopper and mix with half the sugar. Sift remaining sugar with the dry ingredients. Combine beaten egg, milk, and melted butter, and add dry ingredients. Stir only until blended. Fold in sweetened cranberries. Bake in buttered muffin pan in hot oven (425° F.) about twenty-five minutes. This makes a dozen medium-sized muffins.

STEAMED CRANBERRY PUDDING

One cup flour, one and one-half teaspoons baking powder, one-half teaspoon salt, one-half cup bread crumbs, two-thirds cup finely chopped suet, two-thirds cup coarsely chopped cranberries, one egg, and enough milk or water to make a light dough. Mix the ingredients in the order given. Turn into a well-greased bowl or mold. Cover with waxed paper and steam two hours, never allowing the water to come more than two-thirds of the way up the sides of the mold. Turn out and serve with hard sauce or any good sweet sauce.

CRANBERRY MERINGUE PIE

One and one-half cups sugar, two cups cranberries, one-half cup cold water, one tablespoon flour, two eggs, one tablespoon butter, one-half teaspoon vanilla extract, two tablespoons powdered sugar. Cook sugar and water to a syrup; add the cranberries. Cook until they pop. Cool a little. In a bowl mix the flour and egg yolks until smooth; add three tablespoons of the cooked cranberry juice, then add to the berries and simmer for three minutes. Stir in butter and vanilla and set aside to cool. Turn filling into previously baked deep pie crust; cover with a meringue made from stiffly beaten egg whites and powdered sugar. Place in cool oven to set and slightly brown the meringue.

CRANBERRY MOLD

Four cups cranberries, one cup water, two and one-half cups sugar. Cook the cranberries and the water together until the cranberries are tender. Strain and add the sugar, stirring until dissolved, but do not boil. Then turn into an earthen or glass mold which has been wet with cold water, and set aside to become firm. Serve cold.

If preferred, individual molds may be used instead of one large one, but do not use molds made of tin or any other metal. This recipe makes enough for six persons.

CRANBERRY JUICE COCKTAIL

Four cups cranberries, four cups water, two-thirds of a cup sugar. Cook the cranberries and water until all the skins pop open—usually in about five minutes. Strain through cheesecloth. Bring the juice to the boiling point and add the sugar, boiling two minutes. Serve cold. For future use place in sterilized bottles, well corked and sealed.

This drink can also be used as a mix with other beverages, and as a base for fruit punches and fruit cups.

WHO made the first cranberry sauce will never be known, but the custom of eating it with meat, especially turkey, is one of the oldest traditional practices in New England. The Indians, who knew and appreciated the wild cranberry, told the colonists about it. To the new arrivals it was a strange fruit, but it did not take the Puritan housewives long to discover that the small red berry with the tart taste had gastronomical possibilities.

150

In 1672, John Josselyn published in London his *New England's Rareities Discovered*, which was based on observations made many years before in America. In the book he says, "Cranberries or bear-berries, because the bears use much to feed upon them, is a small trayling plant that grows in the salt marshes that are overgrown with moss. The berries are of pale-yellow color afterwards red, as big as a cherry, some perfectly round, others oval, all of them hollow with a sour astringent taste. They are ripe in August and September. They are excellent against the scurvey. They are also good to allay the fervour of hoof disease. The Indians and the English use them much, boyling them with sugar to eat with their meat; and it is a delicate sauce, especially for roasted mutton; some make tarts with them as goose berries."

Five years later we find the loyal colonists of Massachusetts Bay sending King Charles the Second a present of ten barrels of cranberries, which one hopes he and the plump beauties of his court enjoyed.

The cranberry existed in a wild state along the seacoast of New England long before the arrival of the Pilgrims, who, because the blossom and stem resembled the head and neck of a crane, called it the craneberry. It still grows wild, not only on the New England mainland, but on the coastal islands as well. Even today the Cranberry Islands near Mount Desert do not belie the name bestowed upon them years ago. To see and taste a wild cranberry is to realize what culture can do. The modern civilized edition of the cranberry is as different from the original as a bayberry candle from a mazda lamp.

Perhaps it was because the lowly cranberry grew wild in what were considered worthless swamplands that Cape Cod people got the notion the fruit had no great value commercially and so made no attempt to cultivate it. At any rate, nothing was done about it for a couple of centuries, and then it was mere accident that led to the discovery of the proper course to pursue in developing it.

Early in the nineteenth century, Henry Hall of Dennis, who had some lowland property on which wild cranberries grew, cut the scrub growth from some sand dunes nearby, inadvertently causing the sand to drift over the vines to a depth of several inches. The sandy covering did not smother the plants; on the contrary, they sprang up through it vastly improved, and produced superior fruit. This is not to say that the wild berry became overnight the cultivated berry we know today, nor that Henry Hall realized the importance of his discovery. But the change in the vines and berries was so remarkable that the virtue of the sand overlay could not be overlooked. Henry Hall had stumbled upon the secret that was to give rise to an important industry.

Still, many years passed before anything further was done. At length, in 1846, Edward Thatcher of

Yarmouth planted an acre and a half of cranberry vines, and that same year Alvan Cahoon, who had seen what the sand treatment had done to the Hall vines, set out several rods to berries at Pleasant Lake in Harwich. This is said to have marked the beginning of the cranberry industry.

Some time was to pass before anyone made any money growing cranberries, but gradually the business began to show a profit, and retired sea captains and others became interested. During this period of experiment the industry developed slowly. About the time of the Civil War, however, it began to gather momentum. In 1855, there were only 190 acres under cultivation, but in 1865 there were 1,074, which yielded over 13,000 bushels of cranberries. The swamps of Cape Cod, which for two hundred years had been considered valueless, were beginning to prove themselves the most profitable farm lands in the region. And the Cape had not only plenty of swamps and ponds, but, blessedly, ample supplies of sand, too.

In such things Cape Cod has always been fortunate. It has had its cycles of prosperity followed by brief letdowns, but as fast as one of its industries has declined another has arisen to take its place. There was the whale fishery, for example, and the salt industry, and the fabulous days of sail. One by one these went by the board, until by 1860 the outlook was again rather bleak. Nobody went to sea any more; the clam flats and the oyster beds remained, but fishing generally was becoming more and more centered in Gloucester and Boston; the summer boarder had not yet reached the Cape. Things were at a pretty low ebb, when presently the tide began to turn. This time it was the cranberry that did it.

Families who had been struggling desperately against poverty, and used the old swamp only to cut peat because they could not afford to buy wood or coal to keep warm, found themselves comparatively well off. The widow with a mite—widows always abound among seagoing people—discovered that the morass behind the house actually paid dividends and wasn't just waste land after all. The sea captain who had been taken aback because he couldn't find a ship plunged into the battle of the bogs and made the turf fly.

In January, 1842, when Charles Dickens arrived at Boston on his first American journey, he apparently encountered cranberries for the first time in his life while staying at the Tremont House. He seems to have been much less enthusiastic about them than his fellow countryman and earlier visitor to America, John Josselyn. "In our private room," he says in his *American Notes for General Circulation*, "the cloth could not, for any earthly consideration, have been laid for dinner without a huge glass dish of cranberries in the middle of the table." And he complains further of the deformed beefsteak with a flat bone in the center that was invariably the principal dish at breakfast.

The cranberries which Dickens mentions could scarcely have been the cultivated article at that time. Nor is it likely that he had ever tasted the berry before. The cranberry familiar to us is a native of this continent alone. Since Dickens's day the cranberry has been grown from American vines on a limited scale in England and Holland.

Our American cranberry plant is an evergreen trailer with numerous upstanding branches that bear the blossoms and the fruit. The runners reach a length of several feet, the uprights a height of four to ten inches. Each upright may produce from one to seven berries. The vines completely carpet the cultivated bog and blossom in late June and early July. The berries, which mature quickly, are ready for harvesting in September and October. By the Fourth of July, when the vines, with their dark green, shiny leaves, are usually in full bloom, the flat expanses of bog have the appearance of beautifully enameled meadows. The bogs do not hold their deep green look the year round, turning brown in winter.

The shape and color of the berries differ according to the variety. Some are round, others oval, some pear-shaped, and still others fusiform. During the course of its career the cranberry undergoes several color changes. At first it is green, turning from that to cream, then to pink, then to light crimson, and lastly, depending on the variety, to the deep red often approaching black. When ripe the varieties range from light to dark red, and some parts of the country favor one color and some another. New York City, for example, likes the dark-colored berry, while Pittsburgh, St. Louis, and many western markets prefer the light-colored fruit, as the more deeply colored berry is considered by them to be overripe. If the growing season is late the berries sometimes have to be harvested before they are fully tinted.

Over ninety per cent of the cranberries grown on Cape Cod are either Blacks or Howes. The early Blacks (named from the dark color of the berry) originated in Harwich. The Howes vine was first cultivated by James Howes of Dennis, who sold hundreds of barrels of cuttings for the planting of new bogs. All varieties grown in the region are indigenous to the soil of the Cape, and improvement has come about by careful selection, transplanting, and cultivation of the best vines.

The word "bog" used in connection with cranberry growing is misleading, as one quite naturally thinks of a bog as a quaggy, spongy place. A cranberry bog, however, is not wet; it is a thoroughly drained piece of ground, with marginal and transverse ditches for drainage and irrigation. Swampland is chosen for growing cranberries because the plants thrive best in a peaty or mucky soil. Preparing a bog for planting involves a lot of work, as all vegetation has to be cleared from the land. Trees, bushes, and underbrush are cut and hauled away, and the stumps gotten out. The top turf is then cut in squares and stripped off, exposing the peat or muck beneath; this is composed of a smooth-textured vegetable mold with an admixture of finer mineral matter. The turf is turned upside down; when thoroughy dry, the soil is shaken out of it and left on the surface of the bog, while the roots and other trash are removed.

After this operation, called scalping, has been completed, the area is graded as nearly level as possible, and then ditched. The periodic floodings to which the bogs are subjected as a protective measure against frost and insects plays such an important part in cranberry cultivation that bogs which are not near a good stream have to be provided with reservoirs and pumps.

The next step is to sand the bog, that is, to cover the surface with a layer of coarse sand three or four inches deep. The sand acts as a check to weeds and moss, and gives the roots a growing medium that drains more easily and aerates better than peat soil. It also acts as a mulch, and by exuding heat at night reduces the danger of frost. A bog has to be resanded every few years. Plentiful and convenient supplies of the proper kind of sand have from the beginning given Cape Cod a great natural advantage in raising cranberries.

Cuttings of vines from bogs in good condition are planted in hills at regular intervals, two or three vines to a hill. The plants are pressed down through the sand to the peat beneath with a wooden or iron dibble. As the vines spread out over the sand, they take frequent root until the entire bog is completely covered. Newly planted vines usually come into bearing the fourth year.

The work of building the bogs was formerly done by hand. Recent developments, such as the use of bulldozers, draglines, cranes, and mechanical vine setters, have made the work easier, though no less costly. The present cost ranges from fourteen hundred to three thousand dollars per acre, plus an additional four to eight hundred dollars an acre to care for the new bog until it begins to bear. Money as well as patience is needed to become a successful cranberry grower, to say nothing of the knowledge and experience. A well-constructed, well-tended bog, however, will last indefinitely. Some of the first bogs built on the Cape, almost a century ago, are still producing.

The usual yield per acre is from twenty-one to forty-one barrels, with some bogs producing more than fifty barrels. The price in recent years has ranged from close to twelve dollars to over thirty-one dollars per barrel.

According to the Massachusetts Agricultural Experiment Station, the acreage under cranberry cultivation has not increased greatly during recent years, but there has been a marked rise in production. This has been chiefly the result of cutting down losses caused by pests and frosts. Merely reading a list of the pests that attack the cranberry makes one wonder how the berry manages to survive until it finds its way at last to our tables. It is a constant war, with different techniques required to repel each invading host. Even air power is used in the fight, with helicopters hovering over the bogs to spray them with insecticides.

The cranberry harvest begins early in September and continues through the third week in October. The different varieties ripen at different times, some reaching full color around Labor Day, others not until six weeks later. The early Black variety is picked first, followed by the later Howes. In ripening on the vines, the cranberries grow larger and sweeter, and if permitted to remain until fully matured, the more abundant will be the yield and the sweeter the sauce.

The threat of frost, however, often makes the harvest season one of anxiety for the growers, because cranberries are particularly sensitive to cold. As an emergency measure the bogs are flooded to protect the fruit, just as they are sometimes inundated in the spring to protect the young shoots and buds, but this is not done unless it is absolutely necessary, because flooding tends to lower the staying quality of the berries and delays the harvest at a time when every day counts. Cranberries are not picked when the vines are wet, and heavy autumn dews and overcast skies may delay picking until late in the morning. Fortunately, the bogs on Cape Cod are in more or less open country, which is less likely to be visited by frost than localities hedged about by high wooded hills. The United States Weather Bureau sends out special radio warnings to the cranberry growers, and the Cranberry Station of the Massachusetts Agricultural Experiment Station supplements the government reports.

Some idea of the magnitude of the cranberry industry in Massachusetts may be gained by the number of persons employed during the harvest season. Counting the scoopers and those who work in the screenhouses and processing plants, it is estimated that approximately 15,000 persons are engaged in handling the crop. When the cranberries were largely picked by hand, harvesting used to be a social event on Cape Cod, with whole communities turning out in force to gather the berries. Men, women, and children proceeded to the bogs in buggies, carryalls, and every sort of conveyance. Picking cranberries is hard work, but Cape Cod folk made a field day of it, with lots of sport and rivalry among the pickers. Now ninety per cent of the harvesters are Portuguese, about a quarter of them women.

During the infancy of the industry all the harvesting was done by hand, and the berries were picked into six-quart pails made especially for the purpose. This original bare-hand method is still used when the vines are young, so that they will not be pulled from their beds when the berries are picked from them. The industry was not very old, however, before someone thought of a quicker way of stripping the vines. For many years now the bulk of the crop has been harvested by means of wooden scoops with long teeth. These scoops are about fifteen inches wide. The ten-inch long teeth are spaced about a quarter of an inch apart to permit the branches to pass between them when the vines are combed. Larger scoops worked with both hands and holding about half a bushel of berries enable the harvesters, kneeling on the vines in long lines across the bogs, to work uninterruptedly for some time before they have to stop to empty their scoops. Mechanical picking machines have been introduced, but the old method of scooping the berries is still the one generally used.

Some cranberry growers pay their scoopers by the hour, offering bonuses to speed up the work; while others prefer to have the picking done by the box, because they believe this draws the experts. An efficient man will scoop as many as fifteen barrels of cranberries in a day. During the season of 1947 the prevailing rate of pay was fifty cents a bushel box. It requires a foreman with a crew of sixteen men to pick a fifteen-acre bog, with thirteen working as scoopers and three as helpers. The helpers keep the pickers supplied with empty boxes and remove the full boxes in pneumatic-tired wheelbarrows, stacking them at the edge of the bog until they are trucked away. This might take two or three days.

Many berries fall to the ground during the picking operation. It is estimated that about one-fifth of the crop is left on the bogs when the picking crews finish. But most of these berries, called "floaters," are saved by immediately flooding the bogs, which. brings the loose berries to the surface. The wind drives the floaters to one side, where they are held together by booms of floating planks. Many floaters which get caught among the vines do not rise, and to release these berries new flat-bottomed "float" boats have been developed. One type of boat is driven by an airplane propeller, another by jets of water beneath the surface, and still another by a stern paddle wheel, the operator in hip boots walking behind the boat and guiding it by two handles like a pushcart. Stirring up the shallow water frees the berries from the tangle of vines below and also clears the bog of trash.

From the bogs the cranberries are taken to ventilated storage warehouses, where they remain until prepared for shipment. From these storage places they are removed to the screening houses. Here they are poured into the hoppers of machines equipped with wire screens to eliminate pieces of vine picked up by the scoops and with blowers to rid the berries of chaff. A series of bounding boards separates the sound from the decayed fruit, and there is a device for grading the berries. Most of the berries are then sorted by hand; this work is done by women. A continuous stream of berries passes before the sorters on moving belts. Green or whitish berries and those showing signs of decay or damage by frost are removed.

Cranberries are perishable. Shipping therefore begins almost as soon as the berries are harvested, the first of the new crop reaching the market on the last day of summer. By October first, about one-fifth of the crop has been shipped. Almost all cranberries were formerly shipped in barrels, and many will remember the open cranberry barrel that stood in the grocery at Thanksgiving time. But now they are shipped in half- or quarter-barrel boxes, the former weighing from forty-seven to fifty-one pounds, the latter from twenty-three to twenty-six pounds, depending on the size and quality of the fruit. Recently, cranberries have begun to be put up in cellophane bags. The boxes are packed firmly, in order to prevent thrashing, since this reduces the lasting quality of the fruit. It is not considered good practice to sort or pack berries during wet weather, when they collect moisture; damp berries are apt to rot in transit. Packing reaches its peak in November, and by

Christmas seventy-five per cent of the crop has been sold and shipped as fresh fruit.

Some growers like to get rid of their cranberries as quickly as possible, accepting a lower price than they could perhaps obtain later in the season. It costs less to sort them early in the season, nor is there the shrinkage which is common in the late-season shipments. Other growers prefer to take these losses, on the chance of higher prices later in the year.

Production figures show that out of 784,700 barrels of cranberries raised in the United States in 1947, Massachusetts, with approximately 15,000 acres under cultivation, grew 485,000 barrels, or more than half the world's supply. The annual Massachusetts crop alone is worth from $5,000,000 to $16,000,000. Wisconsin was second with 155,000 barrels, followed by New Jersey with 81,000, Washington 48,000, and Oregon 15,700. Practically the entire crop is consumed in the United States and Canada, as there is little overseas demand for cranberries.

A large part of the Cape Cod cranberry crop is sold through the co-operative association of the Massachusetts cranberry growers, which is affiliated with similar organizations in other states in the American Cranberry Exchange in New York. Through their co-operatives, the growers process the part of the crop not sold as fresh fruit, and the industry has benefited greatly in the results obtained through improved methods of handling, grading, packing, and distributing the crop. Working together, the growers have been able to advertise extensively and build up a year-round market for a fruit that was once thought of by the consumer only at Thanksgiving and Christmas. New and tempting ways of using cranberries have been devised, as may be seen from the recipes in the preceding chapter, and the public has been made aware of the important healthful properties possessed by the fruit, which among other things is full of vitamin C.

Even in John Josselyn's day, as we have seen, the cranberry was recognized as a preventive of scurvy, and in whaling and sailing days it was common practice for ships to carry a barrel of cranberries packed in cold water. Indeed, anyone now can keep cranberries on hand for summer use by sorting and washing the raw berries, then sealing them in sterilized glass containers filled with cold, boiled water.

The Cape Cod custom of cultivating the cranberry, which began a hundred years ago, has stimulated the appetite, aided the digestion, and lent color and tang to the American holiday menu at Thanksgiving and Christmas. "There can be no doubt," wrote Freeman, the historian of this region, "that Cape Cod has the natural soil and climate to produce the cranberry in all its perfection."

I<small>T IS</small> an old Cape Cod custom to be fond of music. This is perhaps true of maritime populations everywhere, but it seems to have been especially so of the Cape, where both fishermen and seamen loved to lighten their labor as well as their leisure with song.

Music was the cause of much discord on the Cape in the eighteenth century, when there was a great difference of opinion concerning the manner of conducting the musical part of the Sabbath service in the meeting house. The lack of harmony over this question reached such an acute stage in the West Parish of Barnstable in 1726 that the police had to be called in to preserve order. Orleans purchased a bass viol for use in its meeting house in 1810, and this is thought to have been the first musical instrument used in a Cape house of worship. To the music of "Few Happy Matches," the people sang, "Lo, on a narrow neck of land," and that other old hymn containing the lines

"Ye monsters of the briny deep,
  Your Maker's praises spout;
  Up from the deep ye coddlings peep,
  And wag your tails about."

When Edward Kendall, the English traveler, visited Cape Cod in 1807, one of the things that most attracted his notice in the meeting house at Wellfleet, where he attended Sunday service, was the appearance of the leader of the choir, who sat in a large gallery with some twenty singers. The choir master, "arrayed in a printed cotton morning-gown, had placed himself on top of the partition of the pew, one leg being supported by the front of the gallery, and the other lying along the top of the partition." Considering the time and place, the dress and posture of the leader were rather informal. Freeman, the Cape historian, thinks he was probably a town character who in this way sought to magnify his position in society.

In his progress down the Cape, Thoreau overtook two Italian boys at Higgins's Tavern in Orleans; they had walked thus far through the sand, with their hand organs on their backs, bound for Provincetown. His friend Ellery Channing, Thoreau's companion on this journey, has told how during Thoreau's last days, on hearing an organ in the streets, playing some old tune of his childhood he would never hear again, the tears fell from his eyes, and he said, "Give him some money, give him some money."

Thoreau thought it would be a hard lot for the two organ-grinders if the people of Provincetown should shut their doors against them. Whose yard would they go to next? But he concluded that they had chosen wisely to come to the Cape, "where other music than that of the surf must be rare." It was probably not so rare as he imagined, at least not when the fishing fleet was home. There was, for example, Captain O. R. Gross, master and owner of the schooner *Rival* of Truro, who had such a passion for music that his crews were usually made up entirely of musicians. At any rate, in the autumn of 1851, when the *Rival* went fishing to the Bay of St. Lawrence, she had an all-musical crew, consisting, says a contemporary account, of the following:

"Capt. O. R. Gross, violinist, tamborinist, violin-cellist, flutist, singist and pianist; John Jay Watson, violinist, guitarist, pianist, singist, etc.; Hiram S. Buffington, violinist and dancist; Adrian Lufkin, violinist and singist; George Urquhart, violinist; the black cook also manifested a musical taste, but as some one greased his fiddle bow the first night out, it was never known what his special acquirements were. He took the insult so much to heart that he left the vessel at the first opportunity which presented itself."

All went well with the *Rival* and her merry musical crew. They had almost succeeded in getting a fare of mackerel, when they were caught in the frightful gale of October 3, 1851, which because of the great number of American fishing vessels lost, was called the "American Breeze." After a narrow escape from foundering, the *Rival* was driven ashore at Cascumpeque, Prince Edward Island, but the crew managed to get ashore, saving not only themselves but their cherished musical instruments as well. They were taken in by a kindly farmer named Patrick Cahill; that same night at the Cahill home they gave a musical entertainment the like of which the Cahills and their neighbors had never heard before. So delighted were the people with the concert that it gave Captain Gross an idea.

Most of the *Rival's* crew found berths in other vessels and went home, but Captain Gross persuaded John Jay Watson to remain with him and go on a concert tour through the Maritime Provinces. Watson was undoubtedly the best musician on the *Rival*. He was a Gloucester youth who had commenced fishing at the age of eight. At the age of fourteen he was offered a full share if he would go with his brother in the *Garland*. Music enchanted him, and he would listen spellbound to the playing of the fishermen. On board the *Garland* was a sympathetic fiddler who taught young Watson to play a couple of simple tunes—"Auld Lang Syne" and "Haste Thee Winter, Haste Away." Before the trip was over, the owner of the violin had even agreed to sell it to the boy, bow and all, for one dollar. The trip was a failure, however, and much as the lad coveted the instrument, he couldn't buy it.

On returning to port, Watson transferred to another vessel. This trip proved more profitable, and when he got home he lost no time in seeking the owner of the violin, returning in triumph with his dollar purchase under his arm. Another old nautical fiddler gave him lessons, and all Watson's time was now spent in his father's barn scraping away madly. The next time he went fishing he got leave to take his fiddle, and delighted his shipmates with his playing of such tunes as "Roll On, Silver Moon," "Dearest May," and "O Susannah."

A long illness prevented him from fishing for some time, but it did not keep him from his precious fiddle. At length, for his health's sake, it was deemed advisable for him to go on a fishing trip, so in the spring of 1850 he went with Captain David Brown of Gloucester. When a storm came up, they took refuge in Northeast Harbor, Maine, where in company with many other fishermen they rode out the tempest. During a lull in the storm, Watson decided to entertain the fishermen lying together in the shelter of Mount Desert with some music. He had made great headway with his playing, having studied the winter before with Professor Fenollossa of Salem. So now, standing on the deck of the fishing schooner, he presented a varied program of popular homespun stuff and brocaded classical pieces which met with a storm of cordiality.

No sooner had he ceased playing than a boat put off from another vessel, and Captain Gross of the *Rival* came aboard to inquire who it was that had shown such virtuosity on the violin.

"There's the young man," said Captain Brown, indicating Watson.

Of this first meeting with Watson, Captain Gross said afterward, "I looked toward the companionway, and there sat a young man as pale as a ghost, his form emaciated to a painful degree, the results, as I afterwards learned, of his sickness. On his head was an old tarpaulin hat, and his whole makeup was rather unattractive. As soon as I shook his hand and heard him talk about music, his appearance was forgotten. All that I knew, saw, or cared for was the man, and not his apparel. We talked of music, and Watson charmed me with his enthusiasm. At my request, he took up his violin and repeated some of the airs which had before impressed me, and I knew at once that he was a born musician. I made him promise he would come on board my vessel, and stay there until the storm was over. It lasted several days, and proved a season of exquisite enjoyment to us both. I also made him promise to go with me in the *Rival* the next year as first hand."

The following season found Watson with Captain Gross aboard the *Rival*. They made several successful offshore fishing trips before the Canadian voyage which ended in shipwreck. Cape Cod folk considered it an ominous omen when a violin string broke while the instrument was being played, but whether or not any of the fiddling fishermen snapped a string on the *Rival* before she was wrecked, it is now impossible to say.

After the disaster at Prince Edward Island, Captain Gross, who had obtained an engagement to play the organ in a small town the following Sunday, sent Watson ahead to Charlottetown to arrange for their first concert. Watson had programs and posters printed and did a thorough job of advance publicity, scattering programs and sticking up posters all over the place. Gross, on his way to town Monday morning, was amazed to see the barns and fences for miles around blazing with bills announcing that Professors Gross and Watson, the celebrated violinists and vocalists, would give their unique entertainment, etc.

Any fears which the shipwrecked Yankee fishermen may have had concerning their debut were soon dissolved. They were an immediate and great success. The whole town turned out to hear them. The program they presented was a mixed grill, consisting of gems from Mozart and Beethoven intermingled with such familiar numbers as "Yankee Doodle," "Hail, Columbia!" and numerous comic songs and sentimental ballads. By popular request they gave a repeat performance, which proved equally successful, and the pair left Charlottetown with a neat packet of money and the feeling that concertizing was more agreeable than fishing. Crowded houses greeted them everywhere they went, thanks to Watson's flair for publicity. At length they reached St. John, then pushed on to Portland, and finally closed their tour with a grand concert at Gloucester, Watson's home port, which was the most successful of all.

Later, Watson studied the violin in Europe, where the famous violinist, Ole Bull, found him and invited him to spend the summer at his home in Norway, which Watson did. Ole, in recognition of the lad's musical talent, gave him a valuable violin. When the blond Viking violinist came to America for the concert season of 1869-1870, Watson, "a hustling little man," was Bull's advance agent, and his genius for publicity, which had first manifested itself in the Maritime Provinces when he was twenty-one, came into full flower. "Mr. Watson's energy and skill," says Bull's most recent biographer, Mortimer Smith, "were indeed remarkable; in Washington he arranged interviews with President Grant, General Sherman, and almost all the members of the Senate."

Watson became a fairly prominent figure in the musical world of his day. He was president of the National American University of Music and other Liberal Arts in New York. He played the violin and conducted now-forgotten orchestras. There used to be a tradition that a conductor should be a violinist, which gave Professor Watson an advantage over ordinary hornblowers and flautists. He seems also to have had an attractive stage personality. The standard dictionaries of music and musicians, however, generally fail to mention him; I did find him in one in which he is given a couple of lines stating that he was a violinist and conductor, who was born in Gloucester in 1830 and died in Boston in 1902. What became of the fiddling Cape Cod fisherman with whom he made his first concert tour, I have been unable to discover, but doubtless the trumpets on the other side sounded for him long ago.

In the golden age of sail, many Cape Cod men served in the square-riggers and were familiar with the shanties sung by sailors when engaged in pulling and hauling and other toil aboard ship. These ballads, some of them lightly humorous, deal with sea hardships and sea fights, women and drink. Seamen liked them because they had a great roll and go, and everybody had a chance to swing into the choruses.

Some people have called these sea songs chanteys, deriving the name from the French word *chanter*, to sing. But the form now generally accepted is shanty, the songs having been sung in shanties, perhaps by Southern Negroes; though Joanna Colcord, who is an authority on the subject, thinks the word may be of New England origin. The lumberjacks of Maine lived during the winter in bunk houses called shanties. When the day's work was over, they would sit around the fire and sing, and their songs were called shanty songs. Many of these men went to sea during the summer, taking their music with them; in this way the songs sung aboard ship came to be called shanties. In any case, it is quite certain that shanty did not come from the French.

The virtue of the shanty was that it co-ordinated the work of sailors aboard ship, often in a long strong pull and a pull all together. One popular old hauling song refers to the girls and boys of Cape Cod.

> Cape Cod girls they have no combs,
> Heave away, heave away!
> They comb their hair with codfish bones,
> We're bound for South Australia.
> Heave away, my bully, bully boys!

Another verse contains these lines sung by the shanty man:

> Cape Cod boys they have no sleds,
> They slide down hill on codfish heads. . . .

Many of the shanties were rather ribald. A good shanty man, indeed, was usually gifted in the art of amusing his shipmates by improvising lines that strayed very far from gentility. The best shanties, however, were not necessarily those that were indecorous. One shanty had a line suggestive of the old Cape Cod custom of bundling—"I wish I was in bed with the captain's daughter."

A celebrated whaling song was written by a Cape Cod man, Dr. John Osborn, who was born at Sandwich in 1713, and at nineteen entered Harvard College, where "he was noted as a lively and eccentric genius." His father, Samuel Osborn, was an educated Scotsman, who at first taught school but finally settled in the ministry at Eastham. Dr. Osborn, who was one of a number of distinguished literary physicians in eighteenth-century New England, practiced in Middletown, Connecticut, where he died in 1753. His song of the whale fishery has a salty tang:

When spring returns with western gales,
   And gentle breezes sweep
The ruffling seas, we spread our sails
   To plough the wat'ry deep.

For killing northern whales prepared,
   Our nimble boats on board,
With craft and rum, (our chief regard,)
   And good provisions stored,

Cape Cod, our dearest, native land,
   We leave astern and lose
Its sinking cliffs and lessening sands,
   While Zephyr gently blows.

Bold, hardy men, with blooming age,
   Our sandy shores produce;
While monstrous fish they dare engage,
   And dangerous callings choose.
  .   .   .   .

We view the monsters of the deep,
   Great whales in numerous swarms;
And creatures there, that play and leap,
   Of strange, unusual forms.

When in our station we are placed,
   And whales around us play,
We launch our boats into the main,
   And swiftly chase our prey.

In haste we ply our nimble oars,
    For an assault design'd;
The sea beneath us foams and roars,
    And leaves a wake behind.

A mighty whale we rush upon,
    And in our irons throw:
She sinks her monstrous body down
    Among the waves below.

And when she rises out again,
    We soon renew the fight;
Thrust our sharp lances in amain,
    And all her rage excite.

With joyful hearts we see her die,
    And on the surface lay;
While all with eager haste apply,
    To save our deathful prey.

There was a great deal of singing in the evening among fishing vessels and among the vessels of the apple-tree fleet, which was the Cape name for coasters which never got out of sight of the apple orchards along the shore. No matter how tired the crew might be after a hard day's work, they were never too weary to sing.

Very popular were the ballads, which because

they usually began with the words "Come all ye," came to be called in nautical circles "Come-all-ye's." They commemorated all kinds of events—shipwrecks, large fares of fish, speedy voyages, the fortunes and misfortunes of seafaring life. They were nothing but sentimental doggerel sung to familiar airs, but a good singer with an extensive repertoire of these ballads was a popular person among seamen, with the same high standing as the square-rigger shanty man.

The accordion was by far the commonest musical instrument afloat, and was to be found in all classes of vessels. Next to it came the violin. To the accompaniment of one or the other of these, the Come-all-ye man sang his heartrending ditties. The shanty singer was also sometimes accompanied.

Whistling on board ship was one kind of music that was not tolerated, particularly when the whistler was a landlubber, as this was superstitiously believed likely to bring on a gale. But in a calm a sailor might whistle harmlessly for a breeze, in the belief that his whistling would raise the wind.

In Benjamin Britten's fishing-village opera, *Peter Grimes*, there is a tuba note that suggests a foghorn. The foghorns of Cape Cod are not music to everybody's ears. Those at the lighthouses are outrageously blatant, and the monotonous boom and thump of the lightships on the shoals when it's "thick o' weather" is not suggestive of the horns of elfland faintly blowing. But they are a reminder that the sea is not merely something to sit beside in summer.

TO TREASURE CURIOUS ANTIQUES
AND SANDWICH GLASS

HISTORY lingers in the antique shops of Cape Cod. In the course of a day's march you come upon many of these places, which mingle all kinds of entertainment in every good sense of the word. There are always people who delight in objects which are particularly characteristic of their period—carriage lamps and mustache cups, beaver hats and pistols, old-fashioned dolls and pewter porringers, ancient clocks and ancestral soup tureens. If today more people than ever seem to be interested in antiques, perhaps this feeling for past periods may in part be attributable to a dislike of the present.

How great a role the sea has played in the history of the Cape is suggested by numerous things in the antique shops. At one time or another over a period of years I have noticed ships' wheels and sea chests, marine lamps and lanterns, compasses and telescopes, ships' bells and ship models, carved and painted scrollwork once part of a vessel's decoration, and even figureheads, navigation instruments and charts, and numerous other things of a nautical character.

During the days of sail Cape Cod sea captains brought home foreign curiosities of all kinds from the far holes and corners of the earth. I have seen artificial flowers made of humming birds' feathers from Rio, and from the same place the horny bill of a toucan, which is almost as large as the bird itself. Green parrots, Java sparrows, canaries, and other tropical songbirds were brought back, and one sometimes comes across the old-fashioned cages in which they were kept. Fans of coral and nautilus shells which once graced the mantel in the home of some sea-going Cape family occasionally turn up, as do sandalwood boxes, bead and shell necklaces, curiously carved bracelets, ginger jars, and foreign coins.

Ship models new and old, bottled and unbottled, are fairly common. Making model ships which will go inside bottles is an antique art, and has been a favorite hobby of seamen for hundreds of years. It took from twenty-five to fifty hours to make one of these models, and it helped to while away the time at sea during long spells of calm weather.

To most people, the old sailors' secret—how the ship got into the bottle—is a mystery. Like George III, who could not understand how the apple got inside the dumpling, bewildered parents have been at a loss to explain the secret to their children. The glass was not blown around the model, as some people have supposed. The ship was actually inserted through the mouth of the bottle, with the masts, spars, and rigging collapsed on top of it, ready to be raised into position when inside by means of a piece of string or thread which had been attached to these parts. It was a tricky art.

Sea chests with rope handles find a ready sale because they are of practical use. Decorators like to get hold of them and do things to them; they adorn the lids and fronts with paintings of ships and compass cards, anchors and other nautical gear, and whales, dolphins, and mermaids. Sometimes they carve them. In their original state they were plainly painted and, like any person's luggage, were unmarked save perhaps for the owner's name or initials. On shipboard they were lashed in place by lines passing through the rope handles.

The Cape Cod antique shops are not given over

exclusively to objects associated with the sea. They are stocked mostly with the things you would expect to find at any first-rate New England dealer's; though here, as elsewhere, certain ones have their specialties and run more to one line of antiques than to another. Visiting these Cape shops and attending auctions is usually an instructive and rewarding adventure.

At one time Cape Cod had a factory which turned out hundreds of thousands of antiques. They were not, of course, antiques when they were made, but acquired that distinction later. From 1825 to 1888 glassware was made at Sandwich in enormous quantities and in great variety. Every conceivable kind of object that could suitably be made of glass was manufactured in this Cape Cod town. All kinds of tableware and other things—tumblers, plates, pitchers, cruets, mustards, salts, candlesticks, lamps, chandeliers, decanters, bottles, jugs, inkwells, toy hats, apothecaries' and chemists' supplies, were turned out wholesale at the Sandwich glassworks, in a wide variety of designs and colors. Even sets of children's dishes were made. Connoisseurs have long considered Sandwich glasss to be highly desirable, and a whole literature has grown up around this special field of collecting.

The founder of the Sandwich glass business was a Yankee genius named Deming Jarves, born in Boston in 1790. He devoted all his life to the glass industry. In 1817, he and others bought the property of the Boston Crown Glass Company of Cambridge, and after organizing a new company began the manufacture of flint glass. The difference between crown glass and flint glass is that the former, which is high-grade window glass, is made without lead, while the latter, which can be used for all purposes, is made with lead. Flint glass got its name because when first developed in England it was made with flints; this practice was soon abandoned.

The art of glassmaking was notoriously a secretive business. When Deming Jarves began to manufacture glass, the American industry was laboring under the handicap of not knowing the English secret of obtaining red lead or litharge, an indispensable ingredient of flint glass. But Jarves, who had an exceptional flair for chemistry, set up an experimental lead furnace at Cambridge in 1818, and succeeded at the first trial in discovering the secret. Thereafter for many years he not only supplied the glass industry with litharge, but painters as well with the kind of lead they needed. Jarves continued as superintendent of the Cambridge glass house until 1824, when he quarreled with his colleagues and went off on his own to Sandwich.

He was an able organizer; not long after he decided to make Sandwich his base of operations he began building a factory and homes for his workers. "In 1825," he wrote in his *Reminiscences of Glass-*

Making (1865), "a Flint-Glass Manufactory was established by individual enterprise in Sandwich, Massachusetts. Ground was broken in April, dwellings for the workmen built, and manufactory completed; and on the 4th of July, 1825, they commenced blowing glass—three months from first breaking ground." The following year he formed a company, incorporating it under the name of the Boston and Sandwich Glass Company.

The new company began modestly enough with an eight-pot furnace, each pot holding 800 pounds. The weekly melt did not exceed 7,000 pounds, giving employment to from 60 to 70 hands. The business expanded rapidly. The weekly melt increased from 7,000 pounds to more than 100,000, and the number of workmen to over 500. From a single furnace of eight pots the factory grew to four furnaces of ten pots each. The greatest care had to be taken in preparing the clay pots. They were made on the premises. The makers, who had to tread the clay with their bare feet, looked as if they were dancing in the pots.

Deming Jarves chose Sandwich as the site for his glassworks chiefly because there was wood in abundance close at hand. This fuel was then considered best for glassmaking, and in the country behind Sandwich were thousands of acres of timber. The farmers living in the hilly country south of the town were glad to cut and haul it by ox team to the glass factory at fifty cents a cord. Most of it was small wood, only a few inches in diameter. It was cut in lengths to fit the furnaces and kiln dried. The furnace tenders were called shearers. When they stoked a furnace they were said to shear the fire.

Transportation was another consideration that favored locating the works at Sandwich. There were no railroads in 1825, so the glass factory was built on a tidal creek. This enabled vessels to bring in supplies of sand and anchor directly alongside the plant. It was not until 1848 that the Old Colony Railroad extended its line to Sandwich. When, in the 1850's, the railroad raised its rates, the glass company built a steamer—the *Acorn*—which could make the fifty-mile run to Boston in good time. When coal instead of wood began to be used for fuel, a wharf was built on Buzzards Bay, and the coal reached Sandwich by a short haul of nine miles by rail across the Cape.

In the early days, sand for the New England glass industry was imported from Demerera. It came as ballast in vessels, and was of fair quality. The War of 1812, however, cut off this supply, and for a while sand from the beach at Plymouth was used. As this sand was not up to standard, it was only employed until sand of better quality was discovered at Morris River, New Jersey. Then it was found that a desirable kind could be obtained in Berkshire County, Massachusetts, and this New England sand served for many years. Washed and carefully sifted, it was ready for use when it reached Sandwich. Pure sand was necessary to make clear, brilliant glass. Impure materials were likely to affect the color.

At first, all glass made at the Sandwich works was blown, but within a few years a speedier and cheaper manufacturing process was developed which brought about a radical change in the glass industry and a great increase of business. Instead of blowing the glass into the mold, it was pressed into it. This Yankee invention demoralized the European glass trade, but enabled the Americans to build up a substantial foreign market. A lot of Sandwich glass was shipped abroad.

It is a moot question who should get credit for inventing pressed glass. Deming Jarves claimed he discovered the process, while two glass technicians at the old plant in Cambridge said they did. Apparently experiments had been carried on at Cambridge and at Sandwich simultaneously. Jarves tried to patent a press which he had improved; in the legal dispute between Jarves and the Cambridge workers which followed, Jarves lost his case in court. One of the complaints made against him in his lifetime was that he had a penchant for taking ideas from others and claiming credit for inventions and improvements to which he was not entitled, though the genius of the man is hardly questionable. In the pressed-glass controversy, which became a case of people in glass houses throwing stones, the honors perhaps should be divided equally between Cambridge and Sandwich.

Connoisseurs, of course, prefer blown glass to pressed glass; it is more brilliant and lustrous, and has a better ring. But Sandwich pressed glass was of first-rate quality and because of its design scarcely any of it is now undesirable from the collector's point of view. For many years the head moldmaker and designer at Sandwich was Hiram Dillaway. The molds for pressed glass were made of brass, and the work must have kept him very busy because of the great number of designs used. He used the dolphin motif, a design still imitated in modern glass, with great success.

The art of making pressed glass was brought to the very point of perfection at Sandwich, with raised designs on many of the products, plates, decanters, punch bowls, vases, pitchers, candlesticks, glasses, and lamps. It was the glass lamps of the Sandwich Glass Company—made at first for whale oil and later for kerosene—that relegated the old metal lamps to dusty desuetude on upper shelves. Very popular in their day and still in great request are the historical plates, depicting outstanding persons and events in American history. Most of the so-called Sandwich lacy glass was made before 1840. The lacy effect was achieved by stippling the background of conventional lace designs.

Many bestsellers in the glass trade were originated at Sandwich. It was here that the first cup plates are thought to have been produced. In the days when people emptied the contents of their teacups into the saucers to cool, small cup plates, three or four inches in diameter, were used as coasters for the cups. For more than a quarter of a century they were enormously popular, and undoubtedly saved many tables and much table linen from marks and stains. Some bore the heads of presidents, or statesmen, or historic scenes.

While there is nothing more beautiful than clear transparent flint glass, there was a demand for colored glassware, and the coloring of glass at Sandwich began in the 1830's. Deming Jarves, who was first of all a chemist, did a good deal of experimenting at Sandwich with noteworthy results, particularly in the case of ruby glass. Jarves never hesitated to bring over foreign glassworkers from whom he could learn something. In one case he paid a British expert a fee of $5,000 and expenses to teach the art of making opal glass at Sandwich. The heavy flint glass lent itself admirably to cutting, and quantities of cut glass in varied assortment was made. Etched glass was also in the Sandwich repertory and stacks of it were sold.

This Cape Cod glass was not made for any luxury market, but for the ordinary trade. It was sold in country stores as well as in city emporiums, and the carriage trade liked it as much as the farm-wagon trade.

A crew of glass workers was called a shop, and the foreman a gaffer. At Sandwich, the crews worked in four shifts, twenty hours a day, four days a week. The first shift began at one o'clock in the morning and worked until six. The second shift went on at seven and worked until twelve. At one o'clock the first shift came in again and labored until six. Then the second shift returned at seven to continue until midnight. The week's work ended at six o'clock Friday morning, when the fires were banked until Monday, thus giving the workers, who were well-paid, a forty-hour week and a long weekend.

The small village which Jarves built for his men was called Jarvesville, and a worker could buy a house on the installment plan. When the railroad came to Sandwich, the village was spoken of as being "below the tracks," the town proper "above the tracks." It was a distinction of a social difference, and may perhaps have been the origin of the phrase "the wrong side of the tracks." It is interesting to note that, before the coming of the railroad, the Sandwich Glass Company built its own line extending from the plant down to the shore, a distance of about a mile across the salt marshes, to bring in supplies from vessels too large to come up the tidal creek to the works. This Cape Cod railroad is said to have been one of the earliest in America.

In 1858, Deming Jarves, who seems to have had the mercurial temperament that sometimes goes with genius, left the Boston and Sandwich Glass Company in a huff, and at the age of sixty-eight built another glassworks called the Cape Cod Glass Company not far from the old plant. The opening of the new works was celebrated by a huge clambake, to which everybody in Sandwich was invited. To spite his neighboring competitor, Jarves offered to pay higher wages. He really intended the business for his son John, but John died during the Civil War, and on the night of April 15, 1869, Deming Jarves himself finally died in Boston. His superintendent, William E. Kern, who did not learn of his employer's death until the next day, attended to the fires of the Cape Cod Glass Company that night for the last time. They were never rekindled.

In 1888, the workers of the Boston and Sandwich Glass Company, stirred up by labor agitators from Pittsburgh, went on strike. They were warned by the management that if they persisted the plant would close down permanently, but they did not believe it. Many had spent their lives, as their fathers had before them, working for the glass company, and to them it was an institution destined to be there a long time. But they were mistaken. The factory was closed and was never reopened. None of the attempts to revive the art of glassmaking in Sandwich proved successful. The only place you can get Sandwich glass today is in the antique shops.

THERE were so few farm animals in New England in early colonial times that very little tallow was available for candlemaking. Deer suet and bear grease were used on Cape Cod, but there was never enough to go round. Imported candles were scarce and expensive. Yet the settlers were not left wholly in the dark. Illumination was derived at first largely from burning pitch-pine knots. Plentiful supplies of this candlewood were to be found on the

Cape, but as an illuminant it was not so satisfactory as candlelight. The pine smoked and spluttered and dripped. It was so messy, indeed, that it was generally burned in the fireplace.

Explaining the use of these pine lights, a New England minister wrote in 1663, "They are such candles as the Indians commonly use, having no other, and they are nothing else but the common wood of the pine tree, cloven into little slices, something thin, which are so full of the moisture of turpentine and pitch that they burne as clear as a torch."

The Cape is still occasionally lit up by burning pitch-pine. The woods where the trees grow are highly inflammable and they are forever catching fire. There are five observation towers on the Cape from which a sharp watch is kept over the pitch-pine woods.

Despite a statement made in 1630 that, though New England had no tallow for candles, yet because of the abundance of fish it could afford oil for lamps, Alice Morse Earle does not believe lamps were then widely used. The earliest form of lamp, she says, was the so-called Betty lamp, which was nothing more than a tiny grease pot, a shallow receptacle two or three inches in diameter, either round or oval in shape, with a nose an inch or two long. It was generally made of pewter, iron, or brass. This was filled with grease or tallow and a tow or rag wick fixed in it so that the end rested on the nose. The Phoebe lamp was similar, but with the added feature of a small cup below to catch the melting grease.

Rush lights were simply rushes stripped of their outer covering down to the pith and dipped in grease or tallow.

With the growth of the whaling industry in the eighteenth century, spermaceti candles made from the white waxy substance found in the head of the sperm whale were extensively used. Quantities were made at Falmouth, and they became an important item in our export trade with England. In the years immediately preceding the Revolution, some 400,000 pounds of these candles were shipped abroad annually, and the business of making them continued until the decline and fall of the whale fishery in New England. Near the Marine Biological Laboratory in Woods Hole stands the Old Candle House, dating from 1836, where spermaceti candles were made when Falmouth was a candle-manufacturing center. Whales, by supplying oil for lamps and wax for candles, did much to brighten the world in dimmer times.

Spermaceti candles were much better than those made of tallow. They lasted twice as long, burning with a flame four times greater, and they gave a softer, pleasanter light. Sellers of these candles claimed that one spermaceti did the work of three tallow candles. They also said they were cheaper and more agreeable to use. But the claim that they exceeded all others for sweetness of scent when extinguished was not true. For they could not match the clean spicy incense of the candles made of bayberry wax.

Long before they had spermaceti candles the housewives of the Cape made candles from the wax of the evergreen shrub known as bayberry. A New England surgeon is said to have been the first to extract wax from bayberries. From this wax he made a salve with which he performed wonderful things. Writing almost two and a half centuries ago, Robert Beverly described bayberry wax as "a pale brittle wax of a curious green color, which by refining becomes almost transparent. Of this they make candles which are never greasy to the touch, nor melt with lying in the hottest weather; neither does the snuff of these ever offend the smell, like that of a tallow candle; but, instead of being disagreeable, if an accident puts a candle out, it yields a pleasant fragrancy to all that are in the room; insomuch that nine people of ten put them out on purpose to have the incense of the expiring snuff."

Bayberry, also called candleberry or wax myrtle, thrives along the New England shores, especially on Cape Cod. "It takes kindly to the open, sandy soil," says one Cape writer, "where it throws out abundance of huge crooked roots, filling the soft sand like eels in a basket. The trunk is smooth and crooked, usually growing two or three feet, but when in great clusters, favorably located, it often stands as high as a man's head. The leaf is thickish, with a tropical polish much resembling the rhododendron. The berry is light gray, or ash color, smaller than a peppercorn, and clusters thick along the branches. The wood is brittle, cracking like pipestems when trod upon, and emitting an aromatic odor."

Thoreau thought the berries had a spicy smell, like small confectionary. He rubbed them between his hands to get off the pitch he had got on them in the pine woods, and he took a small quantity home with him to Concord, where later he made some tallow. "Holding a basket beneath the bare twigs in April," he wrote, "I rubbed them together between my hands and thus gathered about a quart in twenty minutes, to which were added enough to make three pints, and I might have gathered them much faster with a suitable rake and a large shallow basket. They have little prominences like those of an orange all creased in tallow, which also fills the interstices down to the stone. The oily part rose to the top, making it look like a savory black broth, which smelled much like balm or other herb tea. You let it cool, then skim off the tallow from the surface, melt this again and strain it. I got about a quarter pound weight from my three pints, and more yet remained within the berries."

The harvest season for bayberries is not in the

spring when Thoreau picked them, but in the fall between the middle of September and Halloween. The wax on the berries is then at its best. The value placed on the crop in the candle era is shown by the action taken at Provincetown in 1750, where it was "ordered that no bayberries shall be gathered before September 10th." It was in the autumn that the winter supply of candles was made.

In the large New England towns there were candle shops which made and sold candles. Benjamin Franklin's first job, it will be recalled, was in his father's candle shop in Boston. The elder Franklin, who had come to New England in 1682, was a dyer by trade, but found so little work in that line that he became a tallow chandler and soap boiler. In 1716, at the age of ten, Benjamin was taken from school to help his father. "I was employed in cutting wicks for the candles," he says in his autobiography, "filling the dipping mold and molds for cast candles, attending the shop, going of errands, etc."

He loathed the job and wanted to go to sea, but his father wouldn't let him. Since his older brother John, who had been brought up in the trade, had married and left Boston to open a candle shop of his own in Rhode Island, it looked as if Benjamin was destined to take his brother's place in the family business and follow the career of a tallow chandler. But he could not reconcile himself to this, and at the end of two years his father, fearing that Benjamin would run away to sea if he did not find him a more congenial trade, decided that as the boy showed a strong bent for books he should be a printer.

Notwithstanding the existence of candle shops like the Franklins', most candles were homemade; the task fell on the women as part of the household routine. Great kettles filled with tallow, bayberry wax, or beeswax were swung over the fire. Many farmers kept bees then for the express purpose of obtaining wax for candles with the harvest of honey only a secondary consideration. When the wax or tallow in the kettles had melted, the dipping began.

Dipping candles was a long and tiresome process. The usual method was to suspend six wicks from a small rod. Cattails, which prosper greatly in the marshes of Cape Cod, were used as rods there. Two sticks were placed parallel to each other and slightly apart across the backs of a couple of chairs or benches, and across these sticks the candle rods were laid like the rungs of a ladder, with the wicks hanging down. The candlemaker, taking up each rod in succession, dipped the wicks in the hot tallow or wax and replaced them on the sticks to cool. This was repeated again and again. With each dip a thin coat of wax was added, until at length, after several dozen dippings, the candle was built up to the required size. All the time this was being done a sharp eye was kept on the contents of the kettle; the right temperature had to be maintained so the wax would be smooth but not so hot that it melted the wax which had already adhered to the wick. This meant frequent lifting of the heavy kettles on and off the fire.

The introduction of candle molds saved the housewife a great deal of time and work in making tallow candles. Wax candles, however, still had to be dipped, as the wax contracted in cooling and stuck to the molds. The molds were metal tubes of tin or pewter which came in nests of from two to twenty-four. Two wicks were used for tallow candles. They were hung in place on thin rods or wires laid across the top of the mold and the melted tallow was then poured in around them.

Circulating candlemakers traveled about the country with large nests of molds and a supply of wicking, offering to relieve housewives with grease on hand of the work of making it into candles. They could turn out hundreds of candles in a day.

After a batch of candles had been made they were placed in a special candle box made of wood or tin which protected them against nibbling mice and then were stored in a dark cupboard or closet to prevent discoloration. A current supply was kept in a box in some convenient place not too near the fire, which might soften them.

As the plaited, self-consuming wick was not invented until 1825, lighted candles up to that time required a good deal of attention, and snuffers were used to trim the burnt wick-ends and keep the candles from smoking.

It was to save candles and fuel that courting couples indulged in the old New England custom of bundling. Nowhere in New England, according to Charles Francis Adams, did the custom prevail more generally than on Cape Cod, and he cites Doctor Stiles as saying that the practice was continued there longer than any other place. This puzzled Mr. Adams because down to the year 1825 there was a purer strain of English blood to be found in the inhabitants of Cape Cod than could be found in any English county, and yet no trace of the custom had ever been reported in any part of the mother country. It had prevailed in portions of Ireland, Wales, Scotland, and Holland, but he could not see how it could have found its way as a custom from any of those countries to Cape Cod.

In 1730, Reverend Nathaniel Stone of Brewster wrote, "There is a sad failing in family government, —a wicked practice of young people in their courtships, which I have borne my public testimony against." A Barnstable citizen was fined "for having a child by his wife five weeks and four days before the ordinary time of women after marriage." A Sandwich man was also fined because his child was born thirty weeks after marriage. If these men did not plead guilty, their cases may very well have involved miscarriages of justice. The first divorce on the Cape, incidentally, was granted in 1660. The husband was fined and whipped.

More bayberry candles are made on Cape Cod today than were dreamed of in the olden times, and the work is still largely done by women, but not in the home. Most of them are made in the candle factory at Hyannis, where hundreds of thousands of bayberry candles are hand-dipped every year. The business, appropriately enough, was started by a Cape Cod housewife, Mrs. Mabel Kimball Baker, wife of Walter P. Baker, who forty years ago began making bayberry candles in the kitchen of her home to give as Christmas gifts to her friends. It was a happy inspiration. Her friends were delighted with the clear-burning green candles with the spicy aroma. They begged her to make more and offered to pay for them. So Mrs. Baker found herself gathering bayberries, brewing them in her kettle, and after skimming off the wax, making it into candles to sell in her husband's general store.

The candles proved very popular locally, and gradually the demand for them spread to other places. Pickers had to be sent out to gather the berries and the Baker kitchen became crowded with women making bayberry wax and dipping candles. The kitchen still exists, lost somewhere amid the series of low, rambling buildings that comprise the present-day candle plant. Mr. Baker soon saw that candle-making offered a better opportunity for the future than keeping a village store, so he sold his own business and with Mrs. Baker organized the Colonial Candle Company.

The sale of bayberry candles continued to increase, but the greatest stride was made when a way was devised to make solid-color hand-dipped paraffin candles. Colored candles were not new, but those on the market were nothing but white candles dipped in color; when the covering coat chipped off, showing the white beneath, the candles looked as if the rats had been at them. The Bakers were the first to make solid-color candles.

People continue to bring bayberries to the candle factory, where the wax is tried out. Wax is also purchased from anyone who will make it. In small lots, the berries, with twice as much water as berries, are boiled hard for four hours and set aside to cool. After cooling, the wax is removed. It is then melted and strained through cheesecloth. Twelve quarts of berries weighing approximately six pounds make one pound of wax, and thousands of pounds of it are used.

The candles are made a dozen at a time, with the wicks suspended in a frame for dipping. Bayberry candles can be dipped in colder and thicker wax than paraffin candles. By watching the wax and keeping it the right consistency, twenty to twenty-five dips is sufficient, while thirty-five are necessary for hot paraffin candles. The latter are made with soft wax for the inside, about twenty dips, and a hard wax for the outside, about fifteen dips. Then when the candle is lighted the inside burns faster and the harder outside wax forms a cup. This makes a more nearly dripless candle, which is superior to the molded or machine-made kind.

Dipping bayberry candles is a relic of the dark ages on Cape Cod, but in these days of low-key interior lighting the old mild lustre of the candles is appreciated and the custom of making them still lives.

MASHPEE is unique among Cape Cod towns. It is the only one that has kept its Indian name, and it is still chiefly occupied by descendants of the original Cape Indians. There is only one other Indian town like it in Massachusetts, and that is Gay Head on the farthest end of the neighboring island of Martha's Vineyard. Mashpee, with a population of 380, also has the distinction of being the Cape's smallest town, though it is twice the size of Gay

Head, which can boast of only 158 inhabitants. The Gay Headers, however, are of purer racial stock than the Mashpees, who have received infusions from other strains, principally Negro and Portuguese, so that the present population is of mixed lineage, but with many still showing marked Indian characteristics.

The Indian tribes of the Cape owed allegiance to Chief Massasoit of the Wampanoags, who fortunately for the early settlers proved friendly. An eyewitness account tells what this Indian ruler was like. "He was a very lustie man, in his best yeares, an able body, grave of countenance, and spare of speech; in his Attyre little or nothing differing from the rest of his followers, only in a great Chaine of white bone Beades about his necke; and at it behinde his necke hangs a little bagg of Tobacco, which he dranke and gave us to drinke; his face was painted with a sad red like murray, and oyled both head and face, that hee looked greasily. All his followers, likewise, were in their faces in whole or in part painted, some blacke, some red, some yellow, and some white, some with crosses, and other Antick workes, some had skins on them, and some naked, all strong, tall, all men in appearance."

As for the Indian women, Josselyn says, "The women have very good features, seldom without a come-to-me in their countenance, all black-eyed, teeth very white, hair black, thick, and long; broad-breasted, handsome straight bodies and slender limbs cleanly straight, generally as plump as a partridge, and, saving now and then, of modest deportment."

As is well known, the first newcomers to New England were unopposed by the natives probably because a few years before the region had been swept by a plague which wiped out a large proportion of the native population. It was a mysterious calamity which the Indians had never before experienced. "Villages withered away when the blight fell upon them; tribes were obliterated, and nations were reduced to tribes." How they caught it, found it, or came by it nobody knows. Nor is it known for certain what the disease was that destroyed them. But for the settlers the visitation was nothing short of providential.

An incident that occurred on Cape Cod is also said to have been a contributing factor to the peace of the early years. "A French ship," says a New England historian, "had been cast away on Cape Cod. The crew succeeded in landing, but the Indians, less merciful than the sea, butchered all but three of them. Two were ransomed by Dermer, one of Sir F. Gorges's captains. The other remained with the savages, acquired their language, and died among them. Before his death he foretold that God was angry, and would destroy them, and give their heritage to a strange people. They derided him, and answered boastfully, they were so strong and numerous that the Manitou could not kill them all. Soon after the pestilence depopulated the country. Then came the Englishmen in their ships. The savages assembled in a dark swamp, where their conjurors, with incantations lasting several days, solemnly cursed the palefaces, devoting them to destruction. Thus the English found safety in the superstitious awe of the natives."

For many years the name Mashpee, which is from the Indian Massapee, was called Marshpee, a title with a squelchy, waterlogged sound that was unfair to the town, since it gave the impression that it was swamp country, instead of well-drained forest land. Cutting and selling wood was formerly one of the mainstays of the community. In 1837, the Indians built a small vessel; it was owned partly by some of the Mashpees and partly by some white persons, and was commanded by an Indian. This vessel was used to carry wood to Nantucket.

The Reverend Gideon Hawley, who became pastor of the Indian church at Mashpee in 1758 and continued there for nearly half a century, said, "There is no place I ever saw, so adapted to an Indian town as this. It is situated on the Sound, in sight of Martha's Vineyard; is cut into necks of land, and has two inlets by the sea; being well watered by three fresh rivers, and three large fresh ponds lying in the center of the plantation. In the two salt water bays are a great plenty of fish of every description; and in the rivers are plenty of trout, herring, &c. In the woods, until lately, has been a great variety of wild game, consisting of deer, &c.; and adjacent to the rivers and ponds, otters, minks, and other amphibious animals, whose skins have been sought for, and made a valuable remittance to Europe ever since my knowledge of these Indians."

As a haven for the Cape Indians, Mashpee owed its existence to the foresight of Richard Bourne of Sandwich. Inspired by the work of Eliot, the Indian missionary, Mr. Bourne began evangelizing among the Indians of the Upper Cape about the year 1658. Realizing that if his efforts were to produce any lasting good the Indians must have some settled place of their own where they could dwell in peace from generation to generation, he procured for them, chiefly at his own expense, deeds to more than ten thousand acres of land near Sandwich. His son, Shearjashub Bourne, later got the deeds confirmed by the court at Plymouth, with a clause in restraint of alienation, "so that no part or parcel of these lands might be bought by, or sold to, any white person or persons, without the consent of all the Indians, not even with the consent of the General Court."

By 1670, Bourne had made such progress with his band of praying Indians that he was ordained the first pastor of the Indian church at Mashpee. Eliot was present at the ordination. When King Phillip's

War broke out, the people of the Cape were apprehensive, but as a result largely of the missionary work of Mr. Bourne and Mr. Treat of Eastham— he of the terrific voice—the Cape Indians remained friendly, and none of the peninsula towns was attacked.

Following the death of Richard Bourne in 1685, Simon Popmonet, an Indian preacher, became the leader of the church, continuing in office forty years. He was succeeded in 1729 by Joseph Bourne, a descendant of the first pastor; he resigned in 1742, "complaining much of the treatment the Indians received." Then came Solomon Briant, an Indian, who preached in the native dialect. He was followed in 1758 by the Reverend Gideon Hawley. Graduated from Yale in 1749, before coming to Mashpee he had worked among the Stockbridge Indians in Western Massachusetts. He had also made a missionary journey to the Indians in the Scoharie country. Mr. Hawley was not agreeably impressed at first by the Mashpee Indians. They appeared abject and widely different from the Iroquois. They were dressed according to the English mode, but he thought half-naked savages were less disagreeable than Indians who had lost their freedom.

After Mr. Hawley's death, Harvard College named the Reverend Phineas Fish to be his successor. The practical power to make the appointment resided in the college authorities as trustees of a fund used to support the minister of the Indian church. In 1711, the Reverend Daniel Williams of London made this bequest in his will: "I give the remainder of my estate, to be paid yearly to the college of Cambridge in New England, or to such as are usually employed to manage the blessed work of converting the poor Indians there." From this fund Mr. Hawley received $100 a year and Mr. Fish from $390 to $443. Income from the fund is still used to support the Mashpee church.

Phineas Fish, who, one hopes, was related to that old New Englander, Preserved Fish, was graduated from Harvard in 1811; he was settled, not without some local objection, on the church at Mashpee in 1812. By that time the Indian language was extinct, and the pure-blooded Indians had given way to a race of half-breeds, Negroes, mulattoes, and Hessians. Freeman says that the last Indian of unmixed blood was Isaac Simon, but Dr. Alden, writing in 1814, states, "The last was Samuel Richards who died about 1804-5 at 91, the oldest Indian in the tribe—of remarkably upright gait, tall, well-proportioned, of dignified aspect. He had early been taught to read his vernacular tongue, and owned Eliot's Bible. He had been a religious man many years, and was regarded by Mr. Hawley as steady, honest, well-minded. He and his squaw whose name was Hannah Popmonnet, used to converse in their native tongue;

but there is scarcely an individual left who knows much about the original language of Massapee."

It was said at this time that fondness for an idle, wandering life and strong drink characterized a large proportion of the adult population. But some of the best seamen in the whale fishery were from Mashpee. Apart from a few small gardens, there was practically no agriculture, but a good deal of wood was cut and sold from the communal lands, and the women and old men made baskets, brooms, and other Indian wares, which, with berries, fish, etc., they peddled in the neighboring towns.

Most of the Indians lived in houses. They had been granted leave in 1725 to hire outside help in building. In 1767 Mashpee had twenty-one shingled dwellings, and in 1800 eighty. As noted elsewhere, when the English traveler, Kendall, visited the place in 1807 about the only wigwam left was occupied by an Englishman and his squaw. "These people," Kendall said, "are very superstitious, and very fearful of going about in the dark, in which they are constantly apprehensive of being presented with terrifying visions."

Indian legends abound on Cape Cod. Mention has already been made of Maushope, a local Indian giant, who got sand in his moccasins one night and, emptying them into the sea, formed Nantucket and Martha's Vineyard. Another legend connects him with the fogs that sometimes enshroud the Cape. A fabulous bird of inordinate size, which frequently visited the southern shore and carried off small Indian children, aroused the ire of the giant. Wading into the sea in pursuit of this bird of prey, Maushope came to Nantucket, the existence of which had hitherto been unknown. Here he found the bones of the kidnapped children under a great tree. Feeling in need of a smoke he looked about for some tobacco, but could not find any, and filled his pipe with poke weed instead. Since then fogs have been frequent at Nantucket and on the Cape. When the Indians saw the fog coming they would exclaim, "There comes Maushope's smoke."

Vesting of title to the Mashpee lands in the Indians did not give them the right of local self-government. In 1693 they were placed under guardianship, the guardians being answerable to a board of overseers appointed by the colonial government. This system continued until 1763, when Mashpee was made a district and the Indians were allowed to manage their own affairs. They elected five overseers, two of whom had to be white, as did also the treasurer and clerk, and they were allowed to choose two wardens and one or more constables. At the end of three years, however, the empowering law lapsed, and was not renewed. Mashpee reverted to its old form of government.

Many Indian boys and girls were bound out by the guardians to white families, the boys as farm

hands, the girls as servants. Nothing was done to edu-
cate them. It was not until 1831, when the legislature appropriated four hundred dollars to build two
schoolhouses in Mashpee, that Massachusetts be-
stirred itself in the matter of educating these people.
The Indians claimed that for fifty years before the
coming of the Reverend Phineas Fish not a single
Indian had been taught to read, though a few had
learned on their own.

"In all times past," they declared in one of their
addresses to the government, "the natives have been
regarded only as savages. If their children were
taken by the authorities and put out to work, it was
with an understanding that they need not be
schooled, and that they had generally been badly
fed, badly lodged, badly clad. That, though thus deprived of all mental culture, robbed, as has been al-
leged, of their rights, they were constantly subject
to the unfeeling accusation of being degraded."

The Mashpees fought well during the Revolution.
In one regiment alone there were twenty-six of these
Indians. One was named Nocake, another Tumpum.
Many lost their lives, and at the end of the war there
were seventy widows in Mashpee. According to Mr.
Hawley, most of the women lost their husbands and
as a result there was a good deal of mating with
Negroes. These were not newcomers to the Cape,
having been there a long time. Near Truro is a place
named for Congo Pomp, an unhappy slave, who to

sustain himself on the journey he meant to take, placed a jug of water and a loaf of bread under the bough of a tree, and then hanged himself from the limb. John Bacon, a Barnstable lawyer, directed in his will that his Negro slave Dinah should be sold and the proceeds used to buy Bibles for his grand-children. Beau Flash was the nickname of the pic-turesque and notorious Captain Matthias Rich of Truro, who made a fortune dealing in "Guinea blackbirds."

In spite of the excellent showing made by the Mashpees in the war, all former laws relating to the government of the place were repealed in 1788, and a board of white overseers placed over "the Indian, mulatto and negro proprietors and inhabitants of Mashpee," who were thus stripped of their civil rights. Guardians with extensive powers were ap-pointed by the overseers. The Indians protested at being reduced to a state of pupilage, and in 1795 a committee of the legislature investigated the state of affairs at Mashpee. This led to some modification of the law the following year, though not enough to satisfy the Mashpees.

Finally, after trying for years to get their wrongs redressed, the Indians took drastic action. At a coun-cil meeting held at Mashpee on May 21, 1833, a strongly worded set of resolutions was drawn up, which read as follows:

"Resolved, 1. That we, as a tribe, will rule ourselves, and have the right to do so; for all men are born free and equal, as says the Constitution of our country.

"Resolved, 2. That we will not permit any white man to come upon our Plantation, to cut, or to carry off, wood, or hay, or any other article, without our permission, after the 1st of July next."

An address was sent to the trustees of the Williams fund and to the governor and council signed by Ebenezer Attaquin, Ezra Attaquin, and others.

On June 25th they formed a government of their own, giving notice by proclamation to all concerned of the action taken. The proceedings excited the interest of the authorities, and when in July the Indians seized and reclaimed some wood which a white man was attempting to remove from their plantation, the ringleaders were arrested. They were prosecuted for a constructive riot in unloading the wood from the white man's wagon and were convicted and jailed. It was said for the Indians that unloading the wood was like throwing the tea overboard in Boston Harbor.

Undaunted by the imprisonment of their leaders, the Indians next memorialized the legislature in a document setting forth all their grievances and praying for permission to manage their own property, for the abolition of the overseership, and for incorporation as a town, with the power to make their own regulations. A remonstrance to the memorial was signed by Nathan Pocknet and a small minority of thirty-five Indians, to which those who sought freedom, numbering some two hundred and eighty-six men and women, replied that Pocknet was "under foreign influence, and being used by designing men to keep the tribe in bondage."

The Indian delegation that went to Boston made a good impression, and at length in May, 1834, the oppressed Mashpees won their fight for freedom. Mashpee was made a district with powers of local self-government. In 1871 it was incorporated as a town.

In the cranberry-picking season, Mashpees of varying hue may be seen at work on the extensive bogs that are now everywhere.

The Indian church, the Cape's oldest house of worship, where Gideon Hawley, Phineas Fish, and a long line of ministers have preached since the days of Richard Bourne, is still Mashpee's greatest landmark.

TO ATTRACT PERVERSE AND KINDRED SOULS

SOME time ago an anonymous Cape Cod writer called attention in the pages of the *New England Magazine* to the remarkable homogeneousness of the population of Cape Cod. Certain families occupied certain towns and villages. There were the Howes, Searses, and Crowells of Dennis; the Hinckleys and Scudders of Barnstable; the Freemans, Crosbys, and Snows of Brewster; the Nickersons and Smalls of Harwich; the Higginses of Orleans, the

Riches of Truro, and the Atkinses of Provincetown, to name only a few. These families married and intermarried, so that most of the towns and villages were connected by ties of relationship, and the people of the Cape were like one great family whose members lived far enough apart not to quarrel. People called each other by their Christian names, because in the villages where so many had the same family name it was meaningless to say Mr. Bearse or Mr. Eldredge. It was always Uncle John or Aunt Lucy.

Visitors to Cape Cod were then rare, except those who came to see relatives, and strangers were apt to be looked upon with suspicion. Few people had occasion to visit the Cape, which as late as 1870 was said to be a sort of terra incognita to half New England. Yet strangers were always well treated.

When Kendall was there, in 1807, he found that, as usual in little-frequented places, there were no regular inns or public houses, but a large proportion of the inhabitants laid themselves out to give entertainment. Among those who did not, some were prevented by their wealth, but the greater number by their poverty. It was necessary therefore to be directed to a householder of substance. The host or hostess commonly declined to name any sum as payment for the accommodations received, saying that though they entertained people they did not keep tavern. But the traveler knew what he paid elsewhere.

Kendall's journey to Provincetown occasioned a good deal of speculation, particularly among the people of the lower towns, where he was suspected of being on the Cape in connection with a mysterious vessel then lying at anchor in Provincetown Harbor. For six weeks this vessel had filled the town with rumors and even apprehensions. She had come to anchor in the harbor and had shown no signs of departing. Her captain had taken lodgings in the town, but it was rumored that there were passengers on board who never came ashore, but to whom provisions were sent from the town. She was said to have no freight, and the passengers were a man and his wife and family.

Then these particulars came to be doubted, as no information concerning the man and his wife could be learned—where they were born, how long they had been married, etc.—and no reason assigned for their choice of the vessel as their home. Contrary rumors about the freight now gained ground, and from having none at all it was said the hold was full of cannons and stands of arms; that, in short, she was a British vessel, manned by British seamen, and commanded by a British officer; that she had been sent in anticipation of the war that was expected to follow the seizure and impressment of men on board the United States frigate *Chesapeake*, and that her mission was to seize Provincetown and all its flakes and fish when the local fleet returned with the fish. In the meantime, the state of defense of the town was looked at despairingly. Almost every male was absent, and the place had only a couple of small guns among the sand hills.

"The alarm increased," says Kendall, "despatches had been sent to the collector at Barnstable, and to Boston. The collector had long delayed his visit; and it was confidentially whispered, that it had been said in the ship, that the collector would not be allowed to come on board, and that his boat would be received with a broadside. Under these circumstances the captain's accommodation on shore had become a source of complaint; but the family in which he lodged had resisted the popular discontent; and, declaring that he behaved very well, and that they had no doubt all was right, had permitted him to remain: in consequence, there was another rumor, that a quantity of arms had been secretly carried into the house; that the doors and windows were barricaded every night; and that the collector and every other officer of government would be opposed by small arms on shore, not less than by heavy metal in the harbor."

The collector, however, met with no opposition, and came away in the firm belief that the vessel was an American bottom with nothing but what was American on board. Kendall said he had the pleasure of drinking a glass of wine with the captain, a native New Englander, who told him that his vessel had been chartered in the South by the gentleman on board; that he had lain at anchor for some time in a cove at Martha's Vineyard, and that he had come to Provincetown Harbor for better security from the winds. The gentleman by whom he was chartered was a merchant from the South, and his motive for living thus was temporarily to avoid his creditors.

At this time, when visitors to the Cape were rare, a very general prejudice existed among the people living in the hinterland of New England against the inhabitants of Cape Cod. This is said to have arisen from the notion that seafarers as a class were more addicted to vice than others, and also from the wild stories current of the way the Cape people, particularly those in the lower towns, plundered vessels wrecked on their shores and subjected the survivors to inhuman treatment. But if the people of interior New England looked askance at the Cape Codders, no less did the mariners of that region look down on the inland landlubbers.

Timothy Dwight summed up their respective positions in a notable passage which shows him to have been a judicially-minded man.

"A stranger, born and educated in the interior of New England," said the Yale president, "amid the varied beauties of its surface, and the luxuriant succession of its produce, naturally concludes, when he visits Province Town, that the inhabitants and neighbors also must possess a very limited share of enjoyment. Facts, however, refute this conclusion. For aught that we could discern, they were as cheerful, and appeared to enjoy life as well, as any equal number of their countrymen. This, indeed, is easily explicable. Food and clothing, houses, lodging, and fuel, they possess of such a quality, and with so much ease in the acquisition, as to satisfy all the demands of that middle state in life, which wise men in every age have dignified by the name of golden. Nature and habit endear to them the place in which they were born and live, and prevent them from feeling what would be serious inconveniences to a stranger.

"Their mode of life," he continues, "is naturally not less pleasing than that of the farmer and mechanic; for no people are more attached to their employment than seamen. The enterprise, which this life requires, and the energy which it supplies, render it less even and dull, and are probably as well suited to the natural taste of man, as arts or agriculture. The situations of others they rarely see, and therefore are rarely led to make irksome comparisons. The lawn, the meadow, the orchard, and the harvest, excite in their minds neither wishes nor thoughts. The draft of herrings, the fare of cod fish, the conquest of a shark, and the capture of a whale, prompt their ambition, engross their care, and furnish pleasures, as entirely unknown to the farmer, as the joy of harvest is to them. To solitude they are strangers. An active, enterprising life is scarcely molested by ennui.

"Almost every day strangers visit Province Town from different parts of the world; for there is hardly any spot, except great trading cities, which is more frequented by vessels of all descriptions than this. By these they are furnished with business and intelligence, and with not a few of those little varieties in thought and feeling, which contribute so much to the cheerfulness of life. Nor do they fail of enjoying a conscious uninterrupted superiority over mere landsmen. While most of their countrymen have been chained to a small spot of earth, they have traversed the ocean. While the husbandman has followed the plough, or brandished the sickle, the inhabitant of Province Town has coasted the shores of Greenland, swept the Brazilian seas, or crossed the Pacific Ocean, in chase of the whale. Who, that has circumnavigated the globe, will not look down on him, who has scarcely traveled out of his native county, or spent life on his own farm."

The reception of the Pilgrims on the Cape by the Nauset Indians was unfriendly. The first contact with the natives was made by a reconnoitering party of sixteen men under Myles Standish, each with his musket, sword, and corselet. The Indians greeted them with a little April shower of arrows tipped with deer horn, eagle claws, and, strange to say, brass.

Eighteen of the missiles were collected, but a number which fell in the brush could not be found. No one was hurt, and the Indians ran away when Myles Standish let drive at them with his gun which made a prodigious noise that seemed to hang upon the damp Cape air for a long space of time.

This attitude of the Cape Indians toward the newcomers is readily understandable immediately one recalls how still earlier visitors to the New England coast had treated the natives. Cabot kidnapped three savages, taking them to England, where it was said that after a couple of years they could not be distinguished from Englishmen. Weymouth stole five at Pemaquid in 1605. Harlow seized another five in 1611. There were other instances, but the worst outrage of all was Hunt's taking of twenty-four at what became Plymouth, and selling them as slaves in Spain. No wonder the Indians were hostile to the visitors.

The first Christian to die in New England was buried in the sands of Cape Cod. This was one of de Monts's men, who in 1605 met an arrowy death at the hands of the Cape Indians when he tried to recover a kettle one of them had stolen. The following year two of de Poutrincourt's crew were slain by the natives at what is now Chatham, which the French named Port Fortune, in bitter ironical allusion to the misfortunes they had suffered there. Drake says this was the very first recorded collision between Europeans and savages in New England.

Five Frenchmen had, contrary to orders, slept on shore without taking the precaution of maintaining a watch; at dawn on October 15, 1606, the Indians surprised them, instantly killing two. The other three ran to the beach, with the savages in full cry after them.

"Help, they are murdering us!" cried the Frenchmen.

The sentinel on shipboard heard them. *"Aux armes!"* he shouted. "They are murdering our people!"

Without bothering to dress, the ship's company seized their arms and rushed out on deck. Sixteen of them, including the trumpeter and the apothecary, tumbled into the shallop and shoved for the shore. Halted in their progress by a sand bar, they jumped into the cold water and waded a musket shot to the beach. None had stopped to light his match with which to fire his gun, but nevertheless they rushed headlong upon the Indians, who fled precipitately.

It was useless to try to run down the fleet red men among the sand dunes, so the landing party attended to their dead comrades. The preceding day they had erected a cross near the shore, and at the foot of this they buried their deceased shipmates. During the funeral rites the Indians in the distance shouted and danced. Afterward the French returned to their ship and the savages disappeared. This was not the last, however, that the voyagers were to see of the redskins. A few hours later, when the tide was so low it was impossible for the French to get ashore, the Indians returned. Tearing down the cross, they dug up the bodies of the slain men, and in plain view of the ship proceeded to strip them. A bronze cannon on board was fired at them several times, but without effect. The savages threw themselves flat on the ground at each shot. As soon as the tide permitted, the French landed again to re-erect the cross and re-inter the dead, while once more the Indians watched from a safe distance.

When the French withdrew on board a second time, the natives added a final dusty insult. Returning to the beach and turning their backs to the vessel, they derisively threw sand with both hands in the direction of the ship from between their buttocks, at the same time yelling like a pack of wolves. In revenge, the French later killed a number of Cape Indians.

Captain John Smith chided the Pilgrims for wasting time at the beginning of winter exploring Cape Cod. Said this Admiral of New England, to give Smith his proper title, "Yet at the first landing at Cape Cod, being an hundred passengers, besides twenty they had left behind at Plimouth for want of good take heed, thinking to find all things better than I advised them, spent six or seven weeks in wandering up and downe in frost and snow, wind and raine, among the woods, cricks, and swamps, forty of them died, and three-score were left in a most miserable estate at New Plimouth, where their ship left them, and but nine leagues by sea from where they landed, whose misery and variable opinions, for want of experience, occasioned much faction, till necessity agreed them."

The earliest of all New England customs was inaugurated at Cape Cod on Monday, November 13, 1620, old style, when the women of the *Mayflower* went ashore to do the family washing. "Our people went on shore to refresh themselves and our women to wash, as there was great need," says Mourt. Ever since then Monday has been the traditional Yankee washday. This does not mean that the washing was done every Monday; the pioneer women only did it about a dozen times a year, and the custom of the Saturday night bath lagged far behind.

"The washing of linen in New England homes," says Alice Morse Earle, "was done monthly; it is to be hoped the personal baths were more frequent, even under the apparent difficulties of accomplishment. I must state, in truth, though with deep mortification, that I cannot find in inventories even of Revolutionary times the slightest sign of the presence of balneary appurtenances in bedrooms; not even of ewers, lavers, and basins, nor of pails and tubs. As petty pieces of furniture, such as stools, besoms, framed pictures, and looking-glasses are enumerated, this conspicuous absence of what we deem an absolute necessity for decency speaks with a persistent and exceedingly disagreeable voice of the unwashed condition of our ancestors."

Charles Francis Adams said that if among personal virtues cleanliness ranked next to godliness, then it were well if those who lived in New England in earlier days had a sufficiency of the latter quality to make up what they lacked of the former.

Thoreau, speaking of the wooden flakes on which fish were dried, says he saw at several places on the Cape a sort of clothes flakes.

"They spread brush on the ground, and fence it around, and then lay their clothes on it, to keep them from the sand. This is a Cape Cod clothesyard."

There is a pretty old anecdote told in Provincetown of the stranding of the British steamship *Caledonia,* June 1, 1863. She was richly laden with broadcloth, woollen goods, bolts of linen, cotton cloth, etc., much of which was salvaged. While the cargo was being discharged the wreckers and the people on the beach managed to get away with more or less of it for themselves. One night a man employed in the salvaging operations brought home a bolt of Irish linen toweling. As it was stained, his wife washed it, and hung it on the line to dry. But not on her own clothesline. She did not want people to know she had any of the *Caledonia* spoils, so she hung it in the adjoining clothesyard of her neighbor. When it was dry the neighbor took it in, figuring that if she was to have the name of possessing stolen stuff from the *Caledonia,* she might as well have the goods. And the neighbor who had hung out the incriminating wash never dared ask for it.

Samuel Adams Drake, who visited Provincetown ten years later, had some interesting observations to make on the people there.

"With an outward appearance of prosperity," he says, "I found the people bemoaning the hard times. Taxes, they said, were twenty dollars in the thousand, and only ten at Wareham; fish were scarce, and prices low, too, though as to the last item consumers think otherwise. The fishermen I saw were burly, athletic fellows, apparently not more thrifty than their class everywhere. They are averse to doing any thing else than fish, and, if the times are bad, are content to potter about their boats and fishing-gear till better days, much as they would wait for wind and tide. If they can not go fishing they had as lief do nothing though want threatens."

He noticed the familiar Cape names that had been transplanted—Atwood, Nickerson, Newcomb, Rich, Ryder, Snow, and Doane. "In general they are 'likely' men, as the phrase here is, getting on as might be expected of a people who literally cast their bread upon the waters, and live on a naked crust of earth that the sea is forever gnawing and growling at. The girls are pretty. I say it on the authority of an expert in such matters who accompanied me. Not all are sandy-haired."

Like most visitors to the Cape, he could hardly fail to notice the antic spirit of the people. "There is quite a strong dash of humor about these people," says Drake. "They are piquant Capers, dry and sharp as the sand. One of them was relating that he had once watched for so long a time that he finally fell asleep while crossing the street to his boarding-house, and on going to bed had not waked for twenty-four hours. 'Wa'al,' said an old fellow, removing a short pipe from between his lips, 'you was jest a-cannin' on it up, warn't ye?'"

Most writers of the past agreed that the genuine Cape Codders were a handsome race, the men tall, straight, with an aristocratic appearance. The children were attractive, with well-cut regular features. It was easy to see where the Otises, the Quincys, and the Thatchers got their noble looks.

In the course of its history Cape Cod has had some notable ministers. The people of Dennis named the town for their beloved pastor, the Reverend Josiah Dennis, a name since repeated on the east side, west side, and all around the town, for we now have East Dennis, West Dennis, South Dennis, and Dennisport. Freeman, who wrote his history of Cape Cod on the eve of the Civil War, complained because Harvard College had never conferred an honorary degree on a Cape resident, though the towns had from the earliest times been fast friends and efficient supporters of the college. Collegiate honors had been bestowed on many who had left the Cape, but not on anyone living there. The title of D. D., he declared, had been conferred on those who were theological pigmies in the presence of the Cape's great divines.

The voice of one old minister has come down to us across the centuries, namely, that of the Reverend Samuel Treat, the first minister of Eastham, who labored not only among his own people, but also among the Indians in his vicinity, many of whom he converted. When he preached he made the welkin ring. "His voice was so loud that it could be heard at a great distance from the meeting house where he was preaching, even in the midst of the winds that howl over the plains of Nauset." But his preaching was not just sound and fury signifying nothing; it was packed with substantial stuff.

Another minister who did commendable work among the Indians was the Reverend Gideon Hawley, who had the church at Mashpee for nearly half a century; he had been installed as pastor of the Indians there in 1758. A delightfully amusing letter which he wrote in his old age—he died in 1807 at the age of eighty—shows him to have been, like most of the Cape divines, a man with a sense of humor.

"Retired as I am, and at my time of life, I need amusement. I read; but my eyes soon become weary.

I converse; but it is with those who have heard my stale observations and my threadbare stories till they have them by rote. In such a case, what can I do? I walk; but soon become weary. I cannot doze away my time upon the bed of sloth, nor nod in my elbow chair. I, therefore, sometimes sit at the window and view my poultry, after my rural ramble, and relax my mind after studious application.

"These fowls are not very profitable; for they make depredations on all sides, waste the fruits of my fields, and spoil my garden: but I hear their voice hailing the early dawn; and this admonishes me of my duty; —as Inspiration teaches, 'Ask now the fowls, for they will tell thee;' and, in another place, 'Consider the fowls.'

"A very common occurrence attracted my attention the other day: I saw how great an underling one of the cocks was made by the Cockron and others of the flock. He was even deprived of the rights of hens. He dare not sound his clarion, nor associate with the females of the flock! I pitied his fate, and concluded to take an active part in his favor. I fed him from my own hand, and drove away his tyrants, pelting them with stones. This little fellow gathered courage with his strength, sung his notes, and enjoyed his amours in consequence of my favor. But, alas! to the terror and amazement of the whole company, he, in his turn, became an intolerable tyrant! He attacked his sire, and beat the Archon, and wounded one of his fellows of the same brood in such a manner that his life was despaired of; and out of compassion I wrung the neck of the wounded, and lost his carcass. In short, this little cock raised his crest and reigned with a vengeance. I, therefore, laid him under arrest, and kept him in confinement until his passions were cooled. However, it mortified me to consider how inconsiderately I had acted; for it was by my means that this sanguinary affair had been brought about. I did it without any ill design; but it was injudicious. I destroyed the balance of power, and every thing ran in confusion in my republic of hens. The Archon had better understanding, and was wiser in this affair than I was. He saw latent tyranny in the nature of this little fellow; that it would not do to indulge him for he needed a master. However, I have now liberated him from his confinement, and he seems properly humbled, and keeps his rank in life. But I have determined not to meddle in the government of hens in future, nor overturn establishments. Cocks will be cocks. As the sage Indian said, 'Tucks will be tucks, though old hen he hatch 'em.' "

An amusing situation developed when the ladies of the Falmouth church disapproved of the wig worn by their pastor, the Reverend Joseph Metcalfe. He had from time immemorial appeared in a rather dilapidated, frowsy head covering, but visiting Boston he bought himself a stylish new wig, and surprised his congregation by wearing it for the first time the following Sunday morning. His appearance caused a good deal of buzzing, and during the nooning the wig was the chief topic of conversation among the women. Several days later the minister was present at a gathering of the ladies of his congregation, when the wig became the subject of discussion.

"Kindly listening to all their utterances," says a local historian, "and sincerely wishing to know what terms would be granted, he deferentially asked whether he should lay aside the use of a wig altogether? To this they seemed unanimously to object —they would have their minister appear well, but the wig to which they objected had 'an unbecoming look of worldiness and pride.'

" 'Shall I, then, resume the old one, decayed as it is, or will you do me the favor to intimate what alterations are necessary to make the new one a true Christian wig? Come, you, Madame A., just do me the honor to clip off what offends.'

"She hesitated, but he insisted; so a supernumerary lock or two were slightly and delicately clipped.

" 'Is that really all?'

"But others were not satisfied.

" 'Do, then, dear Goodwife B., try to help us, and let us effect this wig's conversion to its proper condition.'

"Mrs. B. suggested only a little additional trimming, and another expert with scissors stood by to execute orders. Nearly all were willing to propose

some improvement and aid in the wig's reformation.
Finally, all but one was satisfied. She had not been
particularly consulted, and had been silent, dissent-
ing only now when she heard the rest of the jury
confess themselves ready for an acquittal of the wig
in its present state from all charge of undue worldli-
ness. She thought the wearing of a wig a breach of
the second commandment. Reverend Metcalfe, however, kindly and meekly obviated her objection,—
suggesting that the wig in its present shape was
really so unlike any thing in heaven above, or on the
earth beneath, or in the waters under the earth that
he thought it could hardly fall under the prohibition
in the decalogue."

It is a conventional gesture of the writers of
travel books to pay tribute to the beauty of the
women of the places they visit. Kendall speaks of
the rural beauties and bonnets "worthy of praise"
that he saw when he attended services at the meeting house in Wellfleet. But Thoreau was not very
favorably impressed by the women of Cape Cod,
though he spoke from limited observation when he
wrote, "A strict regard for the truth obliges us to say,
that the few women whom we saw that day looked
exceedingly pinched up. They had prominent chins
and noses, having lost all their teeth, and a sharp W
would represent their profile. They were not so well
preserved as their husbands; or perchance they were
well preserved as dried specimens."

Later he talked with a singularly masculine woman on the Lower Cape, a Nauset plainswoman, who, he said, was "of a hardness and coarseness such as no man ever possesses or suggests. It was enough to see the vertebrae and sinews of her neck, and her set jaws of iron, which would have bitten a board-nail in two in their ordinary action,—braced against the world, talking like a man-of-war's-man in a petticoat, or as if shouting to you through a breaker; who looked as if it made her head ache to live; hard enough for any enormity. I looked upon her as one who had committed infanticide."

These remarks are hardly flattering to regional vanity, which may account for the fact that when Thoreau's magazine articles about the Cape were collected and published after his death in the volume called *Cape Cod,* the book was not popular with the people or the press of the Cape. But on the whole Thoreau liked the inhabitants. He thought they were forthright and humorous and well-mannered. At Provincetown he was out and about the town before breakfast, talking with the people.

The women of the Cape have always been a valiant race. When the British fleet was threatening Falmouth in the spring of 1779, an enemy marauding party landed one night at Wood's Hole bent on getting fresh supplies of meat, butter, and cheese. Guided by a renegade American, they went to the farm of Manassah Swift, and while most of the party were busy robbing the stalls, pigsties, and henroosts, a detachment went to the house, where Mrs. Swift was alone with her children. Meeting them at the door, she demanded to know if the party had a commander. One of them stepped forward, declaring himself to be the one in charge.

"My house is defended by no man," said Mrs. Swift, "and I have the right to presume that you are a gentleman and will not molest a helpless woman and her children."

The officer then inquired politely if she had any cheese.

"Yes, but no more than for my own use."

He said that he was willing to buy, but she replied that she had none to sell. The renegade with the party then led two of the soldiers to Mrs. Swift's cheese room, where each speared a cheese with his bayonet, intending to march off without paying. But Mrs. Swift stopped them at the door, slipped the cheeses off the bayonets, and placed them in her blue-checkered apron.

"You're a valiant set of fellows, to be sure!" she cried.

And the soldiers slunk out the door without their prizes, and retreated under a withering volley of wholesome advice. The main body was surprised at the beach by the local militia and obliged to put off hurriedly, leaving behind most of the spoils they had collected.

Like the ancient Egyptians who profited by the summer overflow of the Nile, the people of Cape Cod have benefited by the annual summer flood of visitors that inundates the region, though it has proved most advantageous of all to the visitors themselves. There is not a section of the Cape without its special group of enthusiasts to advocate its attractions. Some prefer the seacoast of Bohemia around Provincetown, others perhaps favor a strip of beach or neck of woods possibly miles away, and still others like the atmosphere of a particular old town or village. Not a few are content to take off their shoes and sit beside the sea almost anywhere.

One's choice may be influenced by the good sailing or the good swimming or any one of a great number of other reasons. Daniel Webster, an early summer visitor, said to some Cape friends, "I have always found the air of your country delightful in summer, and there are many sea views remarkably fine; and, I suppose I ought to confess that I did not entirely neglect the streams so highly esteemed by anglers who have thrown the fly in them."

Always hospitable and cordial, the people of the Cape can hardly be blamed if they do not look favorably on all aspects of the summer invasion. They do not, for example, altogether approve of those Provincetown Bohemians who copy the worst features of Greenwich Village life, a view also shared by many summer residents. It is not the hard-working, serious artists whom they regard unfavorably, but those who are only vaguely "artists," persons who are always going to paint or write but never accomplish anything except waste their time in dissolute living. It isn't the school teacher who attends art classes of too short duration and is bent on a little harmless mischief on the side to whom they are averse, but the untidy trousered hussy from Greenwich Village who is up to no good. As one Cape Cod woman said, "I would hate to be caught dead on the streets of Provincetown in the summer."

It used to be said that the Cape was a good place to emigrate from as it held out few inducements to its young people to stay at home; though almost every writer about the Cape has mentioned the warm attachment which the people of the region have for the place of their origin. This feeling existed strongly even in the days of long voyages, when many Cape Codders spent most of their time afloat; through fair weather and foul the population has clung to Cape Cod with rare tenacity. And now people are finding it a good place to migrate to, and many off-Capers have gone there to live the year round.

The sea, of course, has been the dominant influence in the lives of Cape Cod folk. Formerly this was evident in the way the men walked, which was with the gait of mariners, not landsmen, and the sea was in their speech. It still is, to some extent. Cape speech, it has been said, is poetry masquerading as prose.

Whether this is so or not, it is certain that their talk has frequent rainbows in it. It is the people and their way of life quite as much as the romantic land itself that has made Cape Cod one of the most attractive regions of New England.

DATE DUE

GAYLORD   PRINTED IN U.S.A.